Number 133
Spring 2012

New Directions for Evaluation

Sandra Mathison
Editor-in-Chief

Promoting Valuation in the Public Interest: Informing Policies for Judging Value in Evaluation

George Julnes
Editor

PROMOTING VALUATION IN THE PUBLIC INTEREST: INFORMING POLICIES FOR
JUDGING VALUE IN EVALUATION
George Julnes (ed.)
New Directions for Evaluation, no. 133
Sandra Mathison, Editor-in-Chief

Microfilm copies of issues and articles are available in 16mm and 35mm,
as well as microfiche in 105mm, through University Microfilms Inc., 300
North Zeeb Road, Ann Arbor, MI 48106-1346.

New Directions for Evaluation is indexed in Education Research Complete
(EBSCO), ERIC Database (Education Resources Information Center),
Higher Education Abstracts (Claremont Graduate University), SCOPUS
(Elsevier), Social Services Abstracts (CSA/CIG), Sociological Abstracts
(CSA/CIG), and Worldwide Political Science Abstracts (CSA/CIG).

NEW DIRECTIONS FOR EVALUATION (ISSN 1097-6736, electronic ISSN
1534-875X) is part of The Jossey-Bass Education Series and is published
quarterly by Wiley Subscription Services, Inc., A Wiley Company, at
Jossey-Bass, One Montgomery Street, Suite 1200, San Francisco, CA
94104-4594.

SUBSCRIPTIONS cost $89 for U.S./Canada/Mexico; $113 international.
For institutions, agencies, and libraries, $295 U.S.; $335 Canada/Mexico;
$369 international. Prices subject to change.

EDITORIAL CORRESPONDENCE should be addressed to the Editor-in-Chief,
Sandra Mathison, University of British Columbia, 2125 Main Mall,
Vancouver, BC V6T 1Z4, Canada.

www.josseybass.com

Editorial Policy and Procedures

New Directions for Evaluation, a quarterly sourcebook, is an official publication of the American Evaluation Association. The journal publishes empirical, methodological, and theoretical works on all aspects of evaluation. A reflective approach to evaluation is an essential strand to be woven through every issue. The editors encourage issues that have one of three foci: (1) craft issues that present approaches, methods, or techniques that can be applied in evaluation practice, such as the use of templates, case studies, or survey research; (2) professional issues that present topics of import for the field of evaluation, such as utilization of evaluation or locus of evaluation capacity; (3) societal issues that draw out the implications of intellectual, social, or cultural developments for the field of evaluation, such as the women's movement, communitarianism, or multiculturalism. A wide range of substantive domains is appropriate for *New Directions for Evaluation;* however, the domains must be of interest to a large audience within the field of evaluation. We encourage a diversity of perspectives and experiences within each issue, as well as creative bridges between evaluation and other sectors of our collective lives.

The editors do not consider or publish unsolicited single manuscripts. Each issue of the journal is devoted to a single topic, with contributions solicited, organized, reviewed, and edited by a guest editor. Issues may take any of several forms, such as a series of related chapters, a debate, or a long article followed by brief critical commentaries. In all cases, the proposals must follow a specific format, which can be obtained from the editor-in-chief. These proposals are sent to members of the editorial board and to relevant substantive experts for peer review. The process may result in acceptance, a recommendation to revise and resubmit, or rejection. However, the editors are committed to working constructively with potential guest editors to help them develop acceptable proposals.

Sandra Mathison, Editor-in-Chief
University of British Columbia
2125 Main Mall
Vancouver, BC V6T 1Z4
CANADA
e-mail: nde@eval.org

CONTENTS

EDITOR'S NOTES

This issue of *New Directions for Evaluation* is the product of presenta-
tions and sessions I organized at the American Evaluation Association conferences in 2007, 2009, and 2011. The impetus for this work
is the recognition that there is little consensus in the evaluation community
regarding a critical aspect of what we do—what methods should be used to
help judge the *value* of public programs and policies? We make such value
judgments whenever we suggest ways to improve a program or conclude
that one policy is better than another.

This current lack of consensus has been both useful and limiting. Its
usefulness has stemmed from the resulting flowering of diverse approaches
to valuing. However, this default encouragement of diverse methods
becomes more problematic if government and foundation funding begins
prioritizing particular valuing methods as best suited for their decision-
making needs. For example, if a lack of a strong, systematic stance on
valuing methods within the evaluation community results in a more organized paradigm, such as economic valuation, becoming more visible and
preferred for some funded evaluations, proponents and practitioners of
other valuing traditions will feel marginalized and less able to contribute.
Not only will this be unfortunate for some evaluators, it will likely also
result in a distorted understanding of the public interest and a diminished
capacity for evaluation in general to serve this interest.

The evaluation community has been through this before, recently in
response to the priority given in government-funded projects for random-
assignment experimental designs. To vaccinate ourselves even somewhat
from the negative consequences of a conflict on valuing methods, this issue
seeks to promote a dialogue on which of our valuing methods appear most
promising and which works best with whom and under what circumstances.
The goal is for dialogue to lead to some working consensus on multiple
approaches to valuing that would help the evaluation community to speak
with a stronger voice concerning the need to match different valuing
methods with their appropriate contexts.

The issue begins with chapters by Michael Scriven, Marvin C. Alkin
and coauthors, Brian T. Yates, and me that set the context for current
tensions in understanding how we value alternatives. These background

I wish to acknowledge the contributions of anonymous reviewers, Sandra Mathison,
and Debra Rog in providing feedback on the direction and content of this issue. In addition, Debra Rog and Michael Morris helped me give feedback to other contributors to
this issue. As always, remaining flaws are mine.

chapters are followed by two chapters on government evaluation policies, one addressing the methods used at the U.S. Government Accountability Office by Stephanie Shipman, and the other by François Dumaine, providing a contrasting look at recently changing evaluation expectations in the Canadian federal government as a result of its Strategic Review initiative.

The issue ends with several chapters that consider the current theory and research on improving the use of our multiple methods of valuing. Specifically, Eleanor Chelimsky, Michael Morris, George F. Grob, Michael Quinn Patton, and I explore the implications of the ideas in this issue for developing policies that promote context-appropriate valuing in evaluation. I hope the issue promotes constructive dialogues on valuing, to which I also hope you will contribute your views and thoughts.

George Julnes
Editor

GEORGE JULNES is a professor in the School of Public and International Affairs, University of Baltimore, and his work focuses on evaluation methods, particularly for programs targeting disadvantaged and at-risk populations, and also on supporting government policies on evaluation that promote context-appropriate methodologies.

NEW DIRECTIONS FOR EVALUATION • DOI: 10.1002/ev

Julnes, G. (2012). Managing valuation. In G. Julnes (Ed.), *Promoting valuation in the public interest: Informing policies for judging value in evaluation. New Directions for Evaluation,* 133, 3–15.

1

Managing Valuation

George Julnes

Abstract

This chapter introduces some of the challenges in valuing programs and policies that seek to serve the public interest. After examining variations in current practice, the author addresses ways of managing the use of valuing methodologies according to the contexts in which they work best. This, in turn, supports conclusions about desired types of balance in our methods of valuing in the field of evaluation. ©Wiley Periodicals, Inc., and the American Evaluation Association.

Evaluation can be defined simply as "determining the merit, worth, or value of things" (Scriven, 1991, p. vii) or with more detail as "the systematic assessment of the operation and/or the outcomes of a program or policy, compared to a set of explicit or implicit standards, as a means of contributing to the improvement of the program or policy" (Weiss, 1998, p. 4). Either way, an enterprise so defined exists to inform real-world decisions and requires being able to support warranted conclusions about the *value* of what is being evaluated. That is, making real decisions depends on reaching conclusions about whether, for example, an educational program is *good*, is *better* than another, is *worth* the resources required or risks involved,

---

Patria deLancer Julnes and Debra Rog read earlier versions of this chapter and provided helpful feedback. I bear the responsibility for any problems that remain.

or could be *improved* with specified changes. There is, however, little consensus in the evaluation community regarding how we best support these needed conclusions.

This lack of consensus on methods of valuing is becoming more problematic now that (a) evaluation is becoming more central to public-sector decision making and (b) the increasing pressure for evidence-based governance is pushing for more evidence-based, and hence systematic, policies on the methods of valuing appropriate for evaluation, often privileging specific approaches to assessing performance and economic impacts. Some consequences of this pressure for more systematic approaches to valuing are good—evaluators have often been unreflective, and even sloppy, in their approaches to valuing. However, efforts to be systematic often have unintended effects, including premature constriction of useful diversity and a general inflexibility in crafting methodologies to match the needs of specific contexts (Julnes & Rog, 2007; Stake et al., 1997). To respond constructively to pressures for systematization while maintaining the needed flexibility to employ context-appropriate methods of valuing, the evaluation community needs to be proactive in articulating its own working consensus on this issue. This chapter introduces some of the challenges and alternatives to be considered in developing this consensus.

Evaluation as Assisted Valuation

To understand valuing in evaluation is to understand the methods by which we assist our natural abilities to judge the value of alternatives. An example of unassisted valuing could be a common decision where we might prefer a meal that is cheap, tasty, healthy, and convenient. Typically, none of the available options is the best on all four of these criteria, meaning there are pros and cons for each alternative, but we, nonetheless, manage without formal methods to choose what we deem is best. This natural, everyday valuation can be complex but is generally nonproblematic, because the consequences of nonoptimal decisions are minor (Henry & Julnes, 1998).

Essentials of Assisted Valuing

In contrast, when the consequences of a poor decision loom larger, we are often inclined to organize our understanding of the consequences so as to consider the many implications together. That is, we try to assist our natural capacities of valuation, as suggested in a letter from Benjamin Franklin to Joseph Priestley, written September 19, 1772.

> Dear Sir,
>
> In the Affair of so much Importance to you, wherein you ask my Advice, I cannot for want of sufficient Premises, advise you what to determine, but if

you please I will tell you how . . . divide half a Sheet of Paper by a Line into two Columns, writing over one Pro, and over the other Con. . . . If I judge some two Reasons con equal to some three Reasons pro, I strike out the five; and thus proceeding I find at length where the Balance lies. . . . And tho' the Weight of Reasons cannot be taken with the Precision of Algebraic Quantities, yet when each is thus considered separately and comparatively, and the whole lies before me, I think I can judge better, and am less likely to take a rash Step. (Labaree & Bell, 1956)

Franklin's simple explanation addresses most of the essential issues for the current dialogue on valuing policies and programs. First, Franklin acknowledges that the value of his method does not depend on its yielding some exact "Algebraic" answer, only that it reduces the likelihood of our taking "a rash Step." This recognition is particularly relevant for our claim that evaluation can yield warranted valuative conclusions. Second, we can see that Franklin's method is based on *analyzing* the situation (distinguishing important elements, wherein "each is thus considered separately") and then (after eliminating any combinations of pros and cons that seem to cancel each other out) *synthesizing* the elements (combining them in some way, so that "the whole lies before me" and I can see "where the Balance lies") to reach an overall judgment. Significantly, every method used by evaluators for assisting the process of valuation presumes the value of this two-stage approach, though the choices of how to analyze and how to synthesize are points of dispute. After first addressing the warrantability of valuative judgments, these analysis and synthesis stages are addressed in the following sections.

Possibility of Warranted Valuation

The goal of all of these methods of assisted valuation is to yield meaningful judgments of value that support effective decision making. Is it possible for judgments about the value of alternatives to be *warranted* in some meaningful sense, and, if so, how do we support warranted valuation for actions affecting complex societies? For conclusions to be warranted means that there are strong reasons for accepting the claims. The unease with accepting that judgments of value can be warranted stems in part from a long tradition in philosophy and social science of accepting what is called the fact–value dichotomy, the idea that facts (e.g., "the student average on a the test is 86") can be objectively verified and validated, whereas values and value judgments ("this curriculum is better than that one") are subjective and so incapable of validation. As a *dichotomy*, there is no blurring of lines between these two types of assertions—objective, factual conclusions do not depend at all on value judgments and value judgments become strictly a matter of personal preference. If this dichotomy is accepted, if one judgment about value is not, and cannot, be viewed as better than another, then why prefer one methodology for valuing over another?

Fortunately, philosophers and social scientists have largely rejected this dichotomy. Putnam (2002) allows for a *distinction* between most facts and value judgments (there is at least some difference between typical fact and value claims) without accepting a strict dichotomy of the two. Similarly, Hurley (1989) has argued that even if there is no "one best way" of valuing, it is possible for specific value judgments to be warranted. Scriven (this issue) adds to this legitimization of valuing by developing an account of the grounds for concluding that judgments of value are warranted. For social scientists, accepting the warrantability of value judgments depends not on objective truth but on the more pragmatic goal of assisted valuing being able to yield specific judgments about policy or program improvements that can be accepted as actionable as a warranted guide for actions (Julnes & Rog, 2008). If the goal of actionable evidence is to avoid rash actions, then valuation methodologies such as benefit-cost analysis are, indeed, "most plausibly justified on cognitive grounds—as a way of counteracting predictable problems in individual and social cognition" (Sunstein, 2001, p. 233).

Method of Analysis for Valuing

As seen in Franklin's (Labaree & Bell, 1956) distinguishing individual pros and cons, methods of assisted valuing are based on analyzing things in terms of multiple attributes. Further, the attributes distinguished are presumed to be important and capable of evaluative judgment distinct from judgments of other attributes. With Scriven's term *evaluand* used for whatever is being evaluated, the first three steps of his four-step logic highlight one analytic approach (quoted from Fournier, 1995, p. 16; the fourth step involves synthesis, the focus of the next section; see Stake et al., 1997, for an alternative view):

1. Establishing the criteria of merit. On what dimensions must the evaluand do well?
2. Constructing standards. How well should the evaluand perform?
3. Measuring performance and comparing with standards. How well did the evaluand perform?
4. Synthesizing and integrating data into a judgment of merit or worth. What is the merit or worth of the evaluand?

Selecting Criteria for Valuing

The analytic approach to valuing requires distinguishing and selecting the criteria, sometimes thought of as dimensions, on which the thing, the evaluand, is to be judged. For this there are two main sources of criteria, with one justification founded on prescriptive values, claims of what *should* be important based on tradition or authority, and the other on descriptive representation of the expressed values of stakeholders (Shadish, Cook, & Leviton, 1991).

Prescriptive approaches to selecting criteria. Perhaps the most straightforward approach to selecting the valuing criteria to be used in evaluation is to consider the objectives of the policies or programs in question. Although an overreliance on formal objectives has been criticized for taking attention away from other impacts (Scriven, 1993), this approach has a long history and is commonly used by the U.S. Government Accountability Office (GAO) (Shipman, this issue) in valuing both implementation and effectiveness. One obvious advantage to this approach is that the expected activities and outcomes written into legislation and regulations are fairly objective and easy to defend by GAO analysts.

Less official but still traditional is to judge public policy in terms of two prescriptive values, efficiency and equality (Berlin, 1998; Okun, 1975); although improving outcomes regarding both is good, there is generally a trade-off that complicates valuing. Further complicating the trade-offs, freedom, community, security, and privacy are also often promoted as important criteria in valuing public-sector initiatives (Bardach, 2012). Thus, a challenge for prescriptive approaches is justifying which prescriptive values to address with criteria.

In addition to these outcome-based values, many (e.g., Greene, 1994; Morris & Jacobs, 2000) have argued that evaluators need to be concerned with process issues as well. For example, in addition to promoting efficiency and equality, does a program treat participants with dignity, and is a policy consistent with the cultural values of the range of citizens affected? These process issues are often the focus of program advisory boards and so are balanced with the dominant consequentialist stance in evaluation.

Descriptive approaches to selecting criteria. Alternatively, criteria can be selected based on stakeholder input. In addition to many methods, there are whole fields of debate around how best to find out what people really value. Surveys or focus groups can be used to identify, or describe, citizen preferences that can then be used to value alternatives. For example, an approach called contingent valuation uses surveys to develop ratings and rankings of respondent preferences as input for economic analyses (Mitchell, 1989). Alternatively, Stake et al. (1997) recommend in-depth discussions with stakeholders to understand their values. Another tradition extends this emphasis on explication by using a cultural lens to emphasize selected values (e.g., emancipation) and inherent value conflicts, such as the conflict that occurs when evaluation is used as a political tool to impose one set of values on more marginalized groups (Fetterman, 2001). A challenge for descriptive approaches is interpreting the reported values. Are some reported values *needs*, whereas others are merely *preferences* that have reduced claims on public action? What if different descriptive approaches, such as surveys and dialogue-based focus groups, yield different values?

Valuing on Selected Criteria

The second and third of Scriven's four steps of valuing involve judgments about the quality of performance on the selected criteria, referencing the "explicit or implicit standards" noted in the Weiss quote above. When criteria are specified in legislation or regulations, there are often associated standards for rating, or grading, performance, as in saying that 80% of the people eligible for services should receive them or that 70% of students should pass a standardized test. As in the ratings on criteria in *Consumer Reports*, meeting expectations is rated as good; exceeding them is even better.

In the absence of published standards, establishing credible standards is difficult. For example, in a period of high national unemployment, what size of decreased unemployment would warrant judging a responsible policy as "good"? One way to avoid dependence on agreed-upon standards for ratings is to rank the alternatives on the selected criteria. Another approach is to represent performance on criteria in dollar amounts, as when the value of a high school retention project is estimated by calculating the increased lifetime earnings of people who receive a high school diploma. This economic approach to representing values has advantages in appearing objective in the sense of standardized measurement and in matching the financial concerns of many decision makers (Gramlich, 1990; Yates, this issue). However, economic approaches, such as benefit-cost analysis, have their own methodological challenges, reminding us that benefit-cost analysis is an appropriate valuation method in some contexts but should not be supported universally and uncritically by evaluators.

Method of Synthesis for Valuing

It is perhaps telling that the synthesis step in valuing—pulling together the various analytic findings into an overall judgment—is allotted only one of the four steps in Scriven's logic but is nonetheless the source of the most serious challenges. Indeed, as Scriven contends (1993, p. 72), "'Pulling it all together' is where most evaluations fall apart."

Two Challenges for Synthesis

Scriven (1993) and others identify two fundamental challenges for synthesis in valuing—aggregating across multiple criteria and aggregating across many people for public sector initiatives.

Aggregating across multiple criteria. If the alternatives we are considering have contrasting advantages (e.g., one program is a little more effective while the other is substantially less expensive), how do we combine these differing aspects into an overall valuation? Franklin explains his method: "If I judge some two Reasons con equal to some three Reasons pro, I strike out the five." This canceling out of pros and cons (akin to benefits and costs canceling out, referred to as a wash, in benefit-cost analysis) simplifies

NEW DIRECTIONS FOR EVALUATION • DOI: 10.1002/ev

complexity and allows greater focus on what is left (so that "the whole lies before me") to support overall, or aggregate, conclusions. However, there is no consensus on how this aggregation is best done (e.g., Scriven, 1993, p. 72, judges the standard numerical weight-and-sum method to be "invalid"), leaving us to "reckon how to weight opposing values" (Bardach, 2012, p. 37).

Aggregating across individuals. As difficult as it is for individuals to balance competing criteria in judging value, it is even more difficult in valuing policies and programs that purport to serve "public interest." In the middle of the last century economists sought to finesse this difficulty by developing a general method for valuation that would begin with the different preferences of individuals and yield a "social welfare function," based on aggregated rankings of alternatives that provided a straightforward, linear ordering of social preferences. However, Kenneth Arrow demonstrated that even in a simple situation of three alternatives and three stakeholders, there often is no objectively preferable choice: "For *any* method of deriving social choices by aggregating individual preference patterns which satisfies certain natural conditions, it is possible to find individual preference patterns which give rise to a social choice patterning which is not a linear ordering" (Arrow, 1951, p. 330).

Methods of Aggregation

The recognized failure to develop a technical economic approach to aggregated public valuation has not impeded the use of other approaches. The examples provided below show that they differ both in the degree of aggregation and how it is accomplished.

Minimal aggregation. One alternative approach to aggregation is that the "political process takes care of it" (Bardach, 2012, p. 37) so evaluators need only provide impartial background information. For example, GAO analyses generally do not aggregate findings in support of a single summative conclusion, instead often documenting performance separately for multiple groups or on multiple criteria established by regulation or legislation.

Checklist approaches to aggregation. For situations in which summative judgments are deemed appropriate and necessary, evaluators commonly make use of checklists. The task here is to identify the most important criteria for judging value, establish standards, display performance in achieving those standards, as *Consumer Reports* does with its ratings on a few columns of criteria, and reach qualitative or quantitative syntheses of rankings and ratings accordingly. Stufflebeam (2001) used the checklist method to reach overall value judgments about evaluation approaches. Note, however, that checklists are limited in registering and weighting different impacts for different people.

Quantitative aggregation. A third approach to summative conclusions is to aggregate using formal quantitative calculations. For example, *Consumer Reports* not only provides checklists but also generally provides an overall score that is derived from weighting the performance on the identified criteria, ranging from a perfect score of 100 to a perfectly bad score of 0. Multiattribute utility (MAU; Edwards & Newman, 1982) analysis uses stakeholder input to value alternatives on different criteria and weight the criteria to yield a stakeholder-based quantitative aggregation. However, the most dominant quantitative approach to valuing in policy evaluation is economic valuation, which represents the major benefits and costs with the use of a single metric, usually money, that allows aggregation to a single value, as in net present value (Adler & Posner, 2000). Because this approach is generally used to aggregate across many people, it highlights the problem of weighting—should everyone be treated equally so that a $1.10 benefit for a rich person justifies imposing a $1 loss on a poor person?

Social aggregation. A stark contrast to quantitative synthesis, evaluators like Ernie House (House & Howe, 1999) and Robert Stake (Stake et al., 1997) promote a social approach to value synthesis. For House, democratic deliberation is a social process that explicates values and supports judgments. Stake makes use of triangulation and other standard qualitative methods to support disciplined intuition, noting that "we must use intuition as well as analysis to understand the larger picture" (Stake et al., 1997, p. 96). In this perspective, iterative interactions and intuition form the basis of summative judgment.

Prefatory Conclusions

This introductory chapter opened with a call for a more proactive debate in the evaluation community on balancing pressures to be more systematic in using preferred methods of valuing with the need for flexibility in using methods best in specific contexts. This final section addresses the territory of context-aligned valuing and the types of balance among approaches that this issue on valuing, as a whole, needs to support.

Aligning Assisted Valuation With Context

To help structure our thinking about how context should influence methods of valuing in evaluation, Figure 1.1 presents a flow in which (a) various contextual factors result in (b) different understandings of the problems to be addressed through evaluation and the information and process needs of the decisions to be supported. These evaluation needs, in turn, lead to (c) a particular focus for the evaluation and, hence, (d) the methods selected and employed. Elements of evaluation design are addressed elsewhere in this issue, but in reading the chapters that follow, consider the contextual factors that influence the information needs, valuative needs, and social-process needs of particular evaluations. These three categories of needs are not independent, but rather build on each other, with information needs

NEW DIRECTIONS FOR EVALUATION • DOI: 10.1002/ev

Figure 1.1. Relating Evaluation Context to Evaluation Design for Valuing

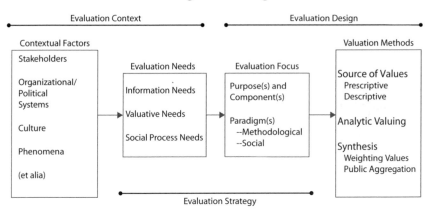

depending on addressing the valuative needs, which in turn presuppose an understanding of the social process that evaluation is intended to serve.

Contextual influences on information needs. Many evaluators follow Patton (2008) in planning evaluations around the information needs of selected stakeholders. Organizational settings (government versus nonprofit; executive versus legislative) and cultural differences (Kirkhart, LaFrance, & Nichols, 2011) influence the nature of these information needs, and so do stakeholder characteristics. Consider Scriven's (1993) delineation of three types of information that an evaluator might provide: (a) reports the *outcomes* and causal *impacts* of a program ("just the facts") and the principal stakeholders use this information to judge the value of the alternatives, (b) offers *conclusions* about the value of alternatives being considered, and (c) recommends specific actions (e.g., to fund or not fund the program). In Scriven's view, the evaluator (almost) never understands enough about the context to recommend actions but, to avoid dereliction of duty, must be the "valuator" who reaches conclusions about the overall value of programs or improvements to them.

I previously presented (Julnes, 1996) a 2 × 2 table distinguishing low and high understanding by the evaluator and low and high valuing capabilities of stakeholders. The logic is that Scriven's position makes sense if the evaluator understands the situation and the stakeholder capability for judging value is low. On the other hand, if the evaluator has a limited understanding of the context and the primary stakeholders are quite capable of interpreting evaluation results, then there are different information needs and the evaluator might interfere by offering valuative conclusions. Notice, however, that this need not be an either–or choice. As Grob (this issue) reminds us, evaluators could legitimately provide conclusions about program value while at the same time supporting stakeholders to do likewise. That is, valuation can be an evaluator contribution without being an evaluator monopoly. Furthermore, no one evaluation culture should monopolize this debate; international evaluation work can sensitize us to cultural issues in aligning the evaluator role in valuing with contexts (Cullen, Coryn, & Rugh, 2011).

Contextual influences on valuative needs. Underlying the more rational information needs of an evaluation are the issues in understanding what people really do value. For fairly concrete issues, such as a city deciding whether to buy or rent equipment, discerning value can be straightforward with reasonable consensus across stakeholders. For initiatives that focus on social outcomes, such as the value of Friday night basketball programs for urban youth, there is generally less consensus on what the criteria of evaluation should be. Further, lack of consensus raises the value-driven question of how divergent values are to be aggregated when addressing the evaluation information needs. This highlights the importance of understanding the different value stances, partly through cultural analysis, and the necessity of group-oriented approaches to valuing.

Contextual influences on social process needs. A final level in Figure 1.1 concerns our understanding of not only the outcomes but also the social processes that evaluation is to support. One aspect is how evaluators and stakeholders co-construct our understanding of our long-term goals in terms of processes. A second issue concerns the paradigms we use to model social and organizational processes in evaluation, how these paradigms give priority to different problems, and how we can be strategic in aligning our use of paradigms with the problems viewed as primary in a particular context.

Managing Balance in Systematization of Methods

Given the increasing importance of evaluation in guiding policy decisions with enormous financial implications, it is natural that policymakers expect the valuation methods in evaluation to be systematic and consistent with best practice. Economic approaches to valuation, such as benefit-cost analysis have, not surprisingly, been accorded a special role in this systemization. Given the myriad choices in aligning evaluations with contexts, it is natural that many evaluators are reluctant to privilege particular methods, such as economic valuation, as a gold standard for valuing. How are we to address these contrasting imperatives?

Balancing analytic and holistic valuing. The two-stage, analysis and synthesis method is often taken for granted, but might something be lost by breaking our understanding down into pieces and then trying to reconstitute, or synthesize, an aggregate judgment? Stake has highlighted this potential problem, contending that the act of identifying criteria artificially elevates certain elements of what is being evaluated (the evaluand), to the detriment of our ability to judge overall value: "Criterial treatment of any evaluand transforms experiential knowledge of it into a knowledge of selected characteristics" (Stake et al., 1997, p. 93).

If analysis into parts fundamentally distorts our judgment, the answer for Stake is to embrace a paradigm that allows our more holistic sense-making abilities greater discretion, noting that whereas "analysis is breaking down to smaller pieces, intuition is pulling hidden patterns together so that we can make better judgments about the evaluand" (Stake et al., 1997, p. 96). This holistic approach to valuing is interesting not only for its contrast with the standard analytic perspective, but also because of its fit with cognitive research that finds asking people to analyze something with the use of separate dimensions actually decreases their competence as evaluators (Wilson & Schooler, 1991).

Balancing systematic and responsive valuing. Building on the balancing of analytic and holistic valuing, the goal for an improved stance on valuing is to be more systematic without becoming rigid, to be able to recognize that different approaches to valuing can be more useful or valuable than others without imposing counterproductive restrictions that constrain effective valuing. This is the challenge in all areas of evaluation as assisted sensemaking, and so, just as evaluation theory and methodology benefited much from efforts to reconcile the contrasting insights of Don Campbell and Lee Cronbach (Shadish et al., 1991), it may be that we need to reconcile the wisdom of people like Michael Scriven and Robert Stake on valuing. In line with the "squaring the circle" metaphor, this reconciliation requires engaging multiple paradigms to suggest policies on valuing that encourage evaluators to balance the systematic clarity of Scriven's logic of valuing with the contextual sensitivity of Stake's responsive evaluation (Julnes, 2010).

Summarizing this need for balance, the evaluation community is confronting an opportunity that is also a problem: An aspect of evaluation, valuation, is becoming increasingly central to the policymaking process, but, without sufficient coherent input from evaluators, government policies may dictate formal methods for judging value that do not reflect our understandings of best practices in specific contexts. To have more input that reflects more of the received wisdom of the evaluation community, we need to develop new frameworks for valuation that are more explicit about the strengths and limitations of different approaches in specific contexts and, hence, can be used to guide decisions about selecting and combining methods to fit differing contexts. The hope for this chapter and the remainder of this issue is that the dialogue begun here will continue and will yield systematic and responsive frameworks for valuing.

References

Adler, M. D., & Posner, E. A. (Eds.). (2000). *Cost-benefit analysis: Legal, economic, and philosophical perspectives*. Chicago, IL: Chicago.

Arrow, K. J. (1951). Alternative approaches to the theory of choice in risk-taking situations. *Econometrica, 19*(4), 404–437.

Bardach, E. (2012). *A practical guide for policy analysis: The eightfold path to more effective problem solving*. Thousand Oaks, CA: Sage.

Berlin, I. (1998). *The crooked timber of humanity*. Princeton, NJ: Princeton University Press.

Cullen, A. E., Coryn, L. S., & Rugh, J. (2011). The politics and consequences of including stakeholders in international development evaluation. *American Journal of Evaluation, 32*(3), 345–361.

Edwards, W., & Newman, J. R. (1982). *Multiattribute evaluation*. Thousand Oaks, CA: Sage.

Fetterman, D. M. (2001). *Foundations of empowerment evaluation*. Thousand Oaks, CA: Sage.

Fournier, D. M. (1995). Establishing evaluative conclusions: A distinction between general and working logic. In D. M. Fournier (Ed.), *Reasoning in evaluation: Inferential links and leaps. New Directions for Evaluation, 68*, 15–32.

Gramlich, E. M. (1990). *Benefit–cost analysis for government programs* (2nd ed.). New York: McGraw-Hill.

Greene, J. C. (1994). Qualitative program evaluation. In N. K. Denzin & Y. S. Lincoln (Eds.), *Handbook of qualitative research* (pp. 530–544). Thousand Oaks, CA: Sage.

Henry, G., & Julnes, G. (1998). Values and realist valuation. In G. Henry, G. Julnes, & M. Mark (Eds.), *Realist evaluation: An emerging theory in support of practice. New Directions for Evaluation, 78*, 53–72.

House, E. R., & Howe, K. R. (1999). *Values in evaluation and social research*. Thousand Oaks, CA: Sage.

Hurley, S. L. (1989). *Natural reasons: Personality and polity*. Oxford, England: Oxford.

Julnes, G. (1996, November). *Establishing value claims in a critical realist world*. Paper presented at the Annual Meeting of the American Evaluation Association, Atlanta, GA.

Julnes, G. (2010). Using research into valuing to enhance the value of rational initiatives to improve performance. In T. Brandsen & M. Holzer (Eds.), *The future of governance: Selected papers from the fifth trans-Atlantic dialogue*. Newark, NJ: National Center for Public Performance.

Julnes, G., & Rog, D. J. (2007). Pragmatic support for policies on methodology. In G. Julnes & D. J. Rog (Eds.), *Informing federal policies on evaluation methodology: Building the evidence base for method choice in government sponsored evaluation. New Directions for Evaluation, 113*, 129–147.

Julnes, G., & Rog, D. J. (2008). Evaluation methods for producing actionable evidence: Contextual influences on adequacy and appropriateness of method choice. In S. I. Donaldson, C. A. Christie, & M. M. Mark (Eds.), *What counts as credible evidence in applied research and evaluation practice?* (pp. 96–131). Thousand Oaks, CA: Sage.

Kirkhart, K., LaFrance, J., & Nichols, R. (2011, April). *Improving Indian education through indigenous evaluation*. Paper presented at the annual American Educational Research Association, New Orleans, LA.

Labaree, L. W., & Bell, W. J. (Eds.). (1956). *Mr. Franklin: A selection from his personal letters*. New Haven, CT: Yale University Press.

Mitchell, R. C. (1989). *Using surveys to value public goods: The contingent valuation method*. Washington, DC: Resources for the Future.

Morris, M., & Jacobs, L. R. (2000). You got a problem with that?: Exploring evaluators' disagreements about ethics. *Evaluation Review, 24*, 384–406.

Okun, A. M. (1975). *Equality and efficiency: The big tradeoff*. Washington, DC: Brookings.

Patton, M. Q. (2008). *Utilization-focused evaluation*. Thousand Oaks, CA: Sage.

Putnam, H. (2002). *The collapse of the fact/value dichotomy and other essays.* Cambridge, MA: Harvard.

Scriven, M. (1991). *Evaluation thesaurus.* Thousand Oaks, CA: Sage.

Scriven, M. (1993). *Hard-won lessons in program evaluation. New Directions for Evaluation, 58.*

Shadish, W. R, Cook, T. D., & Leviton, L. C. (1991). *Foundations of program evaluation: Theories of practice.* Thousand Oaks, CA: Sage.

Stake, R. E., et al. (1997). The evolving syntheses of program value. *Evaluation Practice, 18,* 89–109.

Stufflebeam, D. (2001). *Evaluation models. New Directions for Evaluation, 89.*

Sunstein, C. R. (2001). Cognition and cost–benefit analysis. In M. D. Adler & E. A. Posner (Eds.), *Cost–benefit analysis: Legal, economic, and philosophical perspectives* (pp. 223–267). Chicago, IL: University of Chicago Press.

Weiss, C. H. (1998). *Evaluation: Methods for studying programs and policies.* Upper Saddle River, NJ: Prentice Hall.

Wilson, T., & Schooler, J. (1991). Thinking too much: Introspection can reduce the quality of preferences and decisions. *Journal of Personality and Social Psychology, 60,* 191–192.

GEORGE JULNES *is a professor in the School of Public and International Affairs, University of Baltimore, and his work focuses on evaluation methods, particularly for programs targeting disadvantaged and at-risk populations, and also on supporting government policies on evaluation that promote context-appropriate methodologies.*

Scriven, M. (2012). The logic of valuing. In G. Julnes (Ed.), *Promoting valuation in the public interest: Informing policies for judging value in evaluation. New Directions for Evaluation,* 133, 17–28.

2

The Logic of Valuing

Michael Scriven

Abstract

This chapter outlines the logical infrastructure that makes it possible to claim that one can validate values, both at a general and a context-specific level, other than by direct deduction from other value premises. To make the argument, the author distinguishes between the logic of valuing and the logic of evaluation, the former being the primary focus of the argument, and analyzes the invalidity of the long-standing value-free doctrine in social sciences. The author discusses several ways in which we can establish factual as well as evaluative premises by observation, inference, or definition, that make it possible to infer beyond reasonable doubt to evaluative conclusions. © Wiley Periodicals, Inc., and the American Evaluation Association.

Hume is frequently quoted as having said, "Reason is the slave of the passions." What he actually said was more severe: "Reason is *and ought to be* the slave of the passions *and never pretend to any other office than to serve and obey them*" (italics added). Hume was talking about human passions in the sense of all that we desire or value, not necessarily passionately, and it is clear that as a matter of fact our desires or values include many that can be changed by reason, such as the desire for an electronic gadget, bottled drink, drug, or food, that turns out to have an extremely dangerous design flaw or side effect. Indeed, our desires or values also include *passionate* desires that can and should—at least for most people—be changed by reason, such as the desire for cigarettes or methamphetamine.

So there is a place for reasoning about values, and we even do it, some of the time, and rather obviously should do it more of the time. Hence—if we take him literally—Hume was wrong, both descriptively and prescriptively. A more plausible aphorism in our time of atomic bombs and atomic power plants, biological warfare, global warming, and vanishing natural food and fuel resources, might be: "Reason is often the slave of the passions today *but tomorrow only comes if it rules them.*"

In the profession of evaluation, reason appears to exert some sway over the passions, because our careful investigations to support an evaluative conclusion often appear to weigh one valued outcome against another on the basis of certain factual or purely logical considerations, for example, differential cost or feasibility or consistency. Whether or not there is always an evaluative premise involved, on which Hume's position depends, this is a radical transformation of attitude from the days of the more extreme value-free doctrine about science—most of the 20th century—when reasoning about values and value judgments was held to be impossible within the domain of science; hence program evaluation and other branches of the discipline of evaluation were disbarred from consideration as scientific activities. Although this skeptical conclusion is now widely rejected by social scientists—for example, the social scientists who are authors of a leading text on evaluation define evaluation as applied social science—it is still common, perhaps even dominant, as an underlying prejudice in those disciplines, as we can see from recent anthologies on applied social science in which the term *evaluation* and examples of its practice are entirely absent. What I want to do here is to outline the logical infrastructure that makes it possible to claim that one can validate values, both at a general and a context-specific level, other than by direct deduction from other value premises. To do this thoroughly would take more than the limited number of words than I have, but I can at least indicate the lines of argument that I think are adequate for these purposes.

Preliminaries

We must begin with an understanding of two matters. First, we must understand the distinction between the logic of valuing and the logic of evaluation. The former is our main topic and Hume's topic—the logic of supporting or refuting our commitment to valuing, that is, liking, admiring, or appreciating certain things or tastes or attitudes to which we have become attached. The latter is the logic of the process of applying those likings and valuings to determining the value of *other* things whose value is, for the moment at least, not yet determined or not determined with sufficient certainty for some purpose. These processes are related and overlap in complex ways that we intuit better than we have so far explained, but that should become a little clearer here, where we will use some of the logic of evaluation to get to our conclusions about valuing.

NEW DIRECTIONS FOR EVALUATION • DOI: 10.1002/ev

Second, to get a grip on either of these logics, we need to understand the reasons the value-free doctrine was attractive to both positivists and social scientists in the early decades of the 20th century, and remains so for many social scientists today. The logics of valuing and evaluation exist only because these reasons for denying the legitimacy of both are invalid, and they can be understood and accepted only if we understand the reasons for those errors. I think there were eight main errors involved in the value-free doctrine, of which the first seven were based on an oversimplified philosophy of science inspired by the success of the existing physical sciences, and formulated by the positivists. I'll list them and then indicate why they do not show evaluative claims to be less scientific than the usual scientific claims made by the social scientists proclaiming or still attracted by the value-free doctrine. This will show that the supposed arguments against any logic of valuing or evaluation are flawed, which makes our enterprise here at least possible

First, social scientists thought that the typical value claim was an expression of personal taste, hence entirely subjective in the sense of being idiosyncratic and hence not generalizable—hence not a scientific claim, in their view of science as a discipline primarily interested in general laws and truths, often expressed by saying science was nomothetic rather than idiographic like history. They would often say, "What's good for one person, or valued by one person, isn't good for or valued by another—but that's not the way scientific claims hold true—they're true for all (suitably trained) observers." Their ideal sciences were the great nomothetic sciences, physics and chemistry, but today we are well aware of the virtues of largely idiographic subjects like geology, planetology, forensics, single-subject comparative and clinical psychology, and epidemiology. The positivists thought that idiographic studies were largely prescientific, or merely confirmatory, or anecdotal. And, of course, much of program and personnel evaluation consists of the study of single cases. But this reason is no longer plausible, because single-subject science and idiographic sciences are acceptable.

The second mistake was a kind of reverse edge on the first one, but logically distinct: it was the view that value judgments were also subjective in a second sense, meaning that value judgments could not be confirmed by others (as well as not being true of others). This error was based on a simplistic view of confirmation as direct sensory observation of external phenomena. In fact, other people can confirm claimed matters of taste indirectly by observations of the claimant's behavior, and evidence of his or her veracity in other reports. Both of these errors could have been avoided if they had looked carefully at their own use of value judgments, e.g., in evaluating the work of their students and peers, or in evaluating the experimental designs or scientific instruments they used at work, since those evaluations were supportable by reasons that others could check.

Apologists for the value-free doctrine sometimes say, "Well, what was really meant by *value judgments* was just judgments about ethical and cultural values, which of course *are* like matters of taste and can't be justified by reasons. It's a bad defense because (a) all their arguments were couched in logically general terms, that is, about all value claims, not a subclass; (b) even if there were not good reasons in the abstract for this subset of values, there are plenty of contexts in which there are good reasons for treating them as acceptable premises; (c) context apart, there are plenty of good reasons for or against many, perhaps most, cultural and ethical values (more on this below). The proper defense against illicit smuggling of political values into science is simple; demonstrate their irrelevance if you can. Just don't invent garbage to defend against garbage.

Third, positivists and social scientists had no conception of the way in which the meaning of valuable concepts could be fundamentally context dependent, and still be entirely scientific. Relativity theory had not yet reached the acceptance status of proving that, for example, velocity was fundamentally context dependent, and they didn't think the vast range of context-dependent terms in ordinary language—terms like *tall* or *cheap* or *very large*—was an acceptable type for science. That was an error, and again, scientists' own practice demonstrated that *good* is a highly context-dependent concept, and nonetheless entirely capable of objective use. Their own defense of claims like "General relativity provides a very *good* explanation of some solar eclipse phenomena" or "Einstein was a very *good* theoretical physicist" vitiates the contrary view.

Fourth—the second edge of their objection to terms like *tall* and *cheap*—positivists thought that precision was crucial (or at least very important) for scientific concepts, again not noticing their own use of terms like *original* or *fundamental*, or *analogous*, which have never been quantified. (Today we would add *significant* where the failure of quantification is now enshrined as a great learning opportunity.)

Fifth, a cousin of the fourth mistake, they thought that approximations had no place in laws of nature, although they came around to accepting statistical laws in quantum physics. This was unfortunate, because virtually all the laws positivists used in their examples—the propositions normally called laws in physics and chemistry texts—are in fact only approximately correct, and not very close to the truth across vast ranges of their variables (Scriven, 1961). This rendered invalid one of the objections to the way in which ethical (and other evaluative) generalizations such as "Thou shalt not kill" are maintained in spite of known counterexamples. (The view that scientific generalizations had no exceptions was Karl Popper's favorite hobbyhorse.)

Sixth, positivists had an extremely narrow-minded view of *observation*, and it remains perhaps their most strongly felt as well as their most egregious legacy today. In particular, they would not accept three types of observation that careful commonsense epistemology finds useful and valid: (a) observations of one's own inner states—*introspection*, as in noting the height or depth of one's despair or joy; (b) observation of causation as in seeing someone knock over a cup; and (c) observation of value or merit, as in observing the excellence of a maneuver by a skater, gymnast, calligrapher, mathematician, or soccer player. Obviously one can make mistakes about all of these types of observation, and lie about some of them; but that's true of all observation, which for the positivists was the epistemological foundation of all science: We just have to know how to cross-check, triangulate, and look at the observer's training and track record.

The seventh reason was a naïve concept of *justification*: the idea that for a belief to be justified, it had to be strictly inferred from other beliefs that could be independently established, for example, by observation or logico-mathematical proof. Hence evaluative claims could never be justified, because they could only be inferred from other evaluative claims, which could themselves never be independently justified (since they could never be directly observed, or established as required explanations of what could be directly observed). Of course, once one adopts the commonsense view of what can be observed, we now have to accept factual, observationally verified, evaluative premises, from which we can infer and hence justify some evaluative conclusions in exactly the way the positivists thought impossible.

The eighth factor, a cause but not an explicit belief, and only operative for some of the skeptics about evaluation, was *valuephobia*—the irrational fear of, and extreme opposition to, evaluation that almost every evaluator has encountered in their professional practice. The idea of cutting the wolf loose—legitimating the process of systematic evaluation—understandably made the early social scientists nervous because they were insecure about the credentials of their disciplines.[1] Even today the practice of evaluation, or quality control, is seen as a major threat by many in academia as well as in business or government. Nervousness about evaluation is sensible, criticism of specific approaches to it should be encouraged, but blind opposition is irrational. The sciences are only acceptable as sources of truth as long as their processes of internal verification are valid, that is, they are completely dependent on evaluation for validity. But human nature and nurture make some people supersensitive to criticism, even possible criticism, beyond the point of invading their own survival orientation. It's a phobic reaction.

Probative Proposal

Now let's turn to a more constructive approach and look in more detail at just how we can provide disciplinary and indeed scientific credentials for these imprecise, context-dependent, approximative concepts that are at the heart of evaluation as well as everyday communication. It's good to recall just how this epiphany worked when statistical propositions gradually acquired scientific status, after a beginning during which they were sneered at, even by many mathematicians, as impostors. In just that kind of way, we must extend our logic to handle the new imprecision by (a) specifying the context (e.g., by doing careful needs assessment) instead of throwing up our hands at the fact that context is almost always a key element of the meaning of the very important vocabulary of evaluation; (b) making allowances for inexactitude in our concepts, just as we made allowances for statistical truths, instead of dismissing all vague terms as unacceptable; (c) accepting laws that are only approximations if they bring order out of chaos, that is, exhibit a far-reaching pattern that is close to the truth in many cases of interest, and probably indicative of an underlying microexplanation; and (d) expanding our notion of what is observationally verifiable to include some carefully selected and checked, causal, introspective, and evaluative claims. Spelling out the details of how to make these four adjustments would require more space than we have here, but what are perhaps the two most important moves will be outlined. (e) More controversially, we will need to adopt an extension or modification of what is commonly thought of as the set of permissible inference rules on which all valid reasoning depends. The pinch that the limitation to deduction and statistical inference imposes has long been felt, as one can see immediately from the list of names for some kind of a Third Way that has been proposed.[2] I use the term *probative inference* for my candidate, lifted from the vocabulary of jurisprudence and perhaps slightly extended. It *is* covered by the definition of probative as a legal term in the *Oxford Dictionary of American English*, which is "having the quality or function of proving or demonstrating something," except that I use it by contrast with, rather than as including deduction and probabilistic inference. To place it in the present context, let us go back to the basic logical question that faces any attempt to analyze the logic of evaluation, which is, how can we validate/prove/establish evaluative claims?

The simplest way, already mentioned, is by direct observation, and we'll return to that in a moment. But a more traditional way—in principle—is by providing an evaluative premise that, in conjunction with our empirical premises, makes it possible to deduce the desired evaluative conclusion. (In the technical vocabulary of logic, the premises are then said to entail the conclusion.) The good news for program evaluators is that most evaluations we are commissioned to do only require rather vague evaluative premises that are easy to support, e.g., "The 660,000 tent people in Haiti (as of August 2011) still badly need potable water and more food." Surely it is easy to deduce that the project we are evaluating (the evaluand), which does in fact supply nutritious food and potable water, is valuable. The bad news is that this isn't a deduction, because, among other potential problems, the project may have bad side effects that wipe out the benefits. Well, can't we just check the side effects and then, all being well, add that premise to the others? Unfortunately, checking for all possible side effects is not like checking an integer to see if it's a prime number; it's not a finite task. However good an evaluator you are, and however many possible side effects you have checked for, another adverse one can still show up, years later if not

NEW DIRECTIONS FOR EVALUATION • DOI: 10.1002/ev

immediately. Hence the deduction requires a somewhat speculative premise, without which it is impossible. This example is a really simple one, but even in such a case, getting clear about the evaluative premises it requires is quite valuable, because it underlines that the search for side effects is almost always a crucial part of good evaluation. Given that one rarely finds any sections about side-effect searching in current evaluation reports or textbooks, this is a needed reminder that due diligence requires more attention to them. And that's not the only problem; there may be improprieties, perhaps extremely unethical practices, in the way the water and food is distributed. The benefits may save someone bearing cholera or malice who will kill more people than are saved—not a side effect in the usual sense, but a malign idiosyncrasy. And so on. All that will save the deduction is an illicit circular premise—one that says, "there are no other flaws in the premises—the deduction is valid." Evaluative inference is hazardous if deduction is your ideal. As is much scientific inference.

Nor is a statistical inference possible, meaning by this a quantitative claim. Of course, the more investigation one does, without finding seriously negative side effects, and the more competent at that task one is, the more probable it becomes, in a qualitative sense, that the present project is meritorious. But I think it's advisable not to count that as *statistical* or even *probabilistic inference*, terms that, today, suggest some quantitative scale is being applied or approximated. I am going to take that stand on those terms and demarcate another type of qualitative inference, however, as *probative inference*: It is an inference to a conclusion that has been established, so the utterer claims and is prepared to support, as beyond reasonable doubt. (I am not sure of the extent to which this concept overlaps with defeasible or rebuttable or adbuctive inference, as these terms have been used so far.) This is not inference to a conclusion that is beyond the possibility of error, given the truth of the premises; that would be deduction. But it goes beyond mere probability and it makes a claim of defensibility against attack that goes beyond prima facie status: It issues a kind of promissory note for justified confidence, meaning that further defenses are available if challenged. Under cross examination in a court of law, the expert witness rejects (or should reject), defense counsel's aggressive suggestion that "You just mean 'it's probable, in your view.'" The correct response is: "No, it's not just my view and it's not just probable: it's my professional judgment that the evidence establishes this conclusion beyond any legitimate doubt by an objective, reasonable, and competent expert." Of course, this view is often challenged by other experts produced by the defense—it is indeed rebuttable—and their relative expertise then becomes the focus of attention. But reputation is not enough in the eventual court of scientific inquiry; there must be a specific alternative explanation provided in order to make the challenge credible, and the utterer of the probative claim will have the chance to rebut such a challenge, as the promissory commitment indicates. Absent a successful challenge, we have an inference to the best explanation and good cases of that are good enough to bet one's reputation on—and sometimes, not only in the medical field, to bet one's life on. Their conclusions are not just rebuttable but assertible, and not just assertible but assertible as beyond reasonable doubt.

Moreover, probative inference goes far beyond the domain of explanations: exactly the same epistemology is involved in what we might call inference to the best classification, which we see not only in taxonomy but in the less formal processes of bird-watching, and hieroglyph or bad handwriting interpretation, and even in face and pattern recognition. Indeed, it's clear that it covers inference to the best description. The eliminative and comparative process that goes on in defending a description in a journal, a newspaper, or a scientific report is just like the one that goes on in inference to the best explanation, and both are probative inferences.

The bottom line is that what we have here has essentially the same status as we accord observations, the epistemic gold standard. Observations are also of course fallible, rebuttable, but nevertheless far beyond prima facie truth or mere probability. Although of course a probative conclusion is very highly probable, that's not all it is. It is clear these domains—observation, description, causation, explanation, and evaluation—overlap in their processes of inferential support, and in their eventual certainty status, despite protestations to the contrary. Witnesses do indeed, sometimes, see the defendant shoot the victim dead right in front of them, that is do see, and report as seen, a causal claim: they do not infer to that (Hume was wrong on this, too). Of course, some causal claims *are* inferences but some of these are probative inferences, every bit as beyond reasonable doubt as most observations. For example, when the autopsy reveals only a hole in the forehead and a bullet in the brain—nothing else wrong with the decedent—then the inference to the cause of death is usually probative. This is the informal logic of ordinary inferences and the logic of evaluative inferences, which are part of the folk logic of everyday life at home and in the market and office; and it's not inaccurate talk, it's fully functional and as accurate as is appropriate.

Although one's first reaction to the positivist tightening up of ordinary language is sympathetic, a more sophisticated reaction is a subtler interpretation of that language. One might even come to say that "the whole of science is nothing more than a refinement of everyday thinking. It is for this reason that the critical thinking of the physicist cannot possibly be restricted to the examination of concepts from his own specific field. He cannot proceed without considering critically a much more difficult problem, the problem of analyzing the nature of everyday thinking." Those are the words, spoken in 1936, of a highly credible person who personally knew and was at first much attracted to the positivist position, but came to see beyond it (Einstein, 1936, p. 349).

Is probative inference always the best we can do in supporting evaluative conclusions? John Searle has argued persuasively that there are some cases when one can actually deduce evaluative conclusions from factual premises, for example, when someone borrows money from a friend and says "I owe you fifty dollars" as he takes it—this being a factual, observational, premise—then they really do have an obligation to repay it, and *that* claim is an evaluative deduction from the factual one. These are rare cases, and have not been accepted as incontrovertible cases of deduction—but they are at least cases of probative inference. And there's one more category of probative inferences that is of great importance and very common in evaluation, an explication of one type of inference to the best classification or identification. It is a subcategory of what I call *criterial inference* (Scriven, 1959).

A classical definition is a statement of meaning equivalence between two word strings: (a) the definiendum (the term being defined) and (b) the definiens (the terms making up the definition). Except for mathematical and a few technical terms, and neologisms until they catch on, there are very few valid classical definitions of terms in common use, either in scholarly or in everyday contexts. Nearly all the definitions in a regular dictionary are merely listings of a few leading criteria, that is, properties that are either part of the meaning but not a necessary part of the meaning; or just indicators, that is, properties that are commonly coexistent with the definiendum. And the total list of the terms in the definition does not add to all of the meaning. The term *apple*, for example, is defined in the Oxford American as "the round fruit of a tree of the rose family, which typically has thin red or green skin and crisp flesh." That includes rose hips on a tree rose, which aren't apples, and excludes baked apples, which are. Golden Delicious, a common variety, are yellow, but typically a definition allows for a few exceptions, thereby conceding a lack of general validity. We can improve these definitions by adding more criteria, for example, edibility when ripe, seeds and a core, stems, and so on; but we lose concision and hence convenience, for example, in speed of comprehension, or of lookup (because of increased dictionary size). Criteria are part of the meaning because it's a sample of these that we mention when explaining the meaning of a term to a learner of the language, young or adult. But there are many of them for most common descriptive terms, and few people can even list them all, although they may recognize them as part of the meaning fairly reliably; and they fade away into mere indicators in a gradual and debatable way. If the term X has the indicators C_i, we can express this situation as $X = C_1 + C_2 + C_3 + \ldots$ If this were a classical definition, we could deduce the presence of each of the C's from the presence of X, and the presence of X from the presence of all of the C's. But with criterial definitions, we are considerably limited. We can deduce from X to the conclusion that *some* (unspecified) C's are present, and sometimes we can roughly rank or at least group some of the leading C's in order of the likelihood that they are present in a given context. The winners in this ranking can often be *probatively* but not deductively inferred as present, if X is present. And we can often say that if a specified subset of

C's is present, sometimes the ones in the dictionary, then X is probatively present, and vice versa; those are two important types of criterial inference.

So the claim here is that it is useful to identify a third type of sure inference, along with deduction and very highly probable/statistical inference. The new type is essentially different because it is a pragmatic/rhetorical concept; its meaning is rooted in a potential dialog of challenge and defense that has context-dependent rules. Probative inference has a number of important subtypes: (1) legal reasoning in a criminal court (when the charge is merely a misdemeanor, a lesser standard of proof applies—balance of evidence). This subtype is highly stylized, with explicit rules governing the dialog. (2) Inferences from most laws of nature (or models of phenomena) to specific predictions or explanations—these can't be deductions because the laws are only approximations; (3) inferences to a classification, for example, by a forensic pathologist or birdwatcher; (4) inferences to the best explanation; (5) inferences to evaluative conclusions from some evaluative generalizations (e.g., "Tent people in Haiti badly need food and potable water"); (6) inferences based on very strong analogies or theories, for example, to other minds and other planets; and (7) the fundamental process of induction to the future, which may be another example, but its candidacy would need further support.

Many of the informal logic/critical thinking/argumentation experts would be sympathetic to much of what's just been said. But now we come to something new; it provides us with the eighth strand in a logic of valuing, making up a logic that is rather different from the usual logic of science as represented by philosophers of science even today. (8) When you learn the meaning of a word (call it X) in the usual way—that is, someone tells you, or gives you some examples of what it means (i.e., an ostensive definition), or if you look it up in a dictionary—you have usually learned to associate its meaning with a set of criteria, C_i, with some sense of the relative weight of these. But now I want to suggest that it is a *separate* task, often a longer one, to learn the meaning of good X and/or bad X. For example, it is easy to learn what a mountain bicycle is, or what a word processing program is, but that doesn't tell you the criteria for a good one (though of course you know that set will include the first set). For that you need an expert and/or a research budget plus good product evaluation skills. You don't need all the fine details in order to do serious product evaluation, but you do need at least the section headings in a validated checklist of criteria of merit. (See, for example the checklist of criteria of merit in my professional-level book on evaluating word processors which runs over 35 pages; the section headings would take only four or five pages and are adequate criteria of merit (Scriven, 1983).) Now even a product that scored well on all those criteria could conceivably be seriously flawed; no author is infallible, and technologies change. But anyone who knows the field, even as a consumer rather than a designer, would be likely to agree that a good score on nearly all these dimensions of merit would probatively imply that the product was a very good one.

If the criteria of merit can be defined or explicated nonevaluatively then that inference is an inference from merely factual premises[3] to evaluative conclusions, using only definitional rules for legitimation. Many of these criteria of merit can be so defined; for example, we usually define reliability of office machinery in terms of mean time between failure (MTBF), and we can say, as an example, that an MTBF of 2 years (for failures that take more than 2 hours for the tech service people to fix) rates as good to very good. Because this is part of the meaning of *good word processor*—just as *sweet tasting* is part of the meaning of *good peach* (for out-of-hand eating)—it's not an extra evaluative premise.

Some of the criteria of merit, in real-world checklists, are normally expressed in evaluative language, but that's not important as long as those criteria, in turn, can be defined criterially in nonevaluative language. (This parallels the process of validating theories by appealing to observations; in fact, we often do it by appealing to claims that have a theoretical basis, too, but that's acceptable if they in turn can be validated without assuming the theory at risk.)

To conclude: I think that the preceding material indicates several ways in which we can establish factual as well as evaluative premises by observation, inference, or definition, that make it possible to infer beyond reasonable doubt to evaluative conclusions. Such reasoned inferences establish the truth of conclusions about valuing or disvaluing many things— in certain contexts, and to varying degrees—including passions for addictive drugs, hatred of ethnic groups, and the fundamental ethical attitude of valuing the prima facie rights of all humans (Scriven, 1966). So Hume was wrong, but more importantly, so were many of the reasons we have accepted for believing him.

Notes

1. Indeed, the value-free doctrine appears to have originated in Max Weber's cautions to early sociologists against scientific investigation of government programs, based on his concern about government funding reprisals. That was understandable caution, even if not exactly a testimonial for the search-for-truth value that science is supposed to embody; but the subsequent move to rationalize it with an ill-founded doctrine of value-free science was surely in part valuephobic, as we can see from the extent to which it involved ignoring their own evaluative and scientific practice.
2. New trivalent logics have been called nonmonotonic, default, autoepistemic, paraconsistent, and relevant; the proposed third type of reasoning has been called plausible, prima facie, presumptive, defeasible, analogical (John Wisdom), conductive (Wellman), deduction (Sherlock Holmes), rebuttable (Toulmin), argumentative (Perelman), and the somewhat mysterious abduction (Peirce). (Thanks to Tony Blair for helpful suggestions for inclusion here.) The term *multivalued logic* has been used for a related but not identical amplification of classical logic—the inclusion of more than the two truth values of true and false.

3. What are commonly called *factually true premises*, also known as *matters of fact*, or—speaking slightly more technically—*empirically true premises*, are not, speaking precisely, always nonevaluative, because many evaluative propositions are clearly factual or—at least in one sense—empirical; for example, "Einstein was a great physicist," or "Scoring more than 150 on the usual I.Q. tests, without cheating, means at least that the respondent is an unusually good problem-solver." But here we'll occasionally use the term *factual* (or merely, or purely, or simply factual), or *empirical* (etc.) for brevity, as they are intended colloquially, because they are colloquially meant to convey being nonevaluative. (The false dichotomy of facts vs. values is a relic from the positivists.)

References

Einstein, A. (1936). Physics and reality. *The Journal of the Franklin Institute, 221*(3), 349–382.

Scriven, M. (1959). The logic of criteria. *Journal of Philosophy, 56,* 857–868.

Scriven, M. (1961). The key property of physical laws: Inaccuracy. In H. Feigl & G. Maxwell (Eds.), *Current issues in the philosophy of science* (pp. 91–101). New York, NY: Holt.

Scriven, M. (1966). *Primary philosophy.* New York, NY: McGraw-Hill.

Scriven, M. (1983). *Word magic: Evaluating and selecting word processing.* Belmont, CA: Wadsworth.

MICHAEL SCRIVEN *is a professor of psychology at Claremont Graduate University, a senior research associate at the Evaluation Center, Western Michigan University, and director of institutional research at Palo Alto University. He has served as president of the American Educational Research Association and the American Evaluation Association.*

NEW DIRECTIONS FOR EVALUATION • DOI: 10.1002/ev

Alkin, M. C., Vo, A. T., & Christie, C. A. (2012). The evaluator's role in valuing: Who and with whom. In G. Julnes (Ed.), *Promoting valuation in the public interest: Informing policies for judging value in evaluation. New Directions for Evaluation, 133,* 29–41.

3

The Evaluator's Role in Valuing: Who and With Whom

Marvin C. Alkin, Anne T. Vo, Christina A. Christie

Abstract

The act of valuing in an evaluation may be perceived in different ways. We consider the multiple theoretic perspectives that govern an evaluator's behavior and present a typology of evaluator valuing roles. Within this typology we describe three ways in which value judgments are typically reached—by stakeholders alone, stakeholders and evaluators in consort with each other, or by evaluators only. This heuristic offers a more explicit understanding of how valuing occurs in evaluation. © Wiley Periodicals, Inc., and the American Evaluation Association.

Evaluation scholars and practitioners have dedicated much energy and effort to shaping and defining the program evaluation profession. This observation is evidenced by the array of evaluation theories that are described in the literature and the ongoing research activities and conceptual papers that continue to deepen our understanding of evaluation theory and practice. However, careful review of the program evaluation literature turns up only a few resources that describe value judgments, and operationalize the ways in which they are reached and who is involved in this aspect of the evaluation process.

When considering some of the complexities involved in the valuing process, many issues come to mind. For example, how positive do the findings related to a specific study question have to be to warrant a statement of *good*? Or, conversely, how negative must they be to be considered *bad*? Are criteria sufficiently well established to legitimize such judgments? How are judgments to be made about the overall program given the different value-laden information sources? Additionally, what if the answer to some of the questions (or issues in the evaluation) is good and to others the answer is bad? Are some questions more important than others? How much more important? Just these few questions raise many important issues related to the mechanics of the valuing process. We recognize and appreciate the challenges that accompany difficult-to-make decisions. However, because of page limitations, we have chosen to focus only on those aspects of valuing related to *who* values and how those who are doing valuing are involved in making value judgments. We address these questions. Who decides value? Is it the evaluator who decides? Who else might be involved in the decision?

Michael Scriven has been considered a central figure in calling attention to the role of valuing in evaluation. He argues that, "evaluation is not just the process of determining facts about things (including their effects) . . . [rather] an evaluation must, by definition, lead to *a particular type* of conclusion—one about merit, worth, or significance—usually expressed in the language of good/bad, better/worse, well/ill, elegantly/ poorly, etc." (Scriven, 2003, p. 16). For Scriven, "valuing" is the central component of evaluation and is what distinguishes evaluation from other kinds of systematic inquiry. We, as do many others, agree with Scriven's assertion, which Fournier (2005, p. 140) summarized as: "It is the value feature that distinguishes evaluation from other types of inquiry, such as basic science research."

In a similar vein, Scriven (1986) maintains that it is the evaluator's job to value, to determine whether a program is good or bad. This simple assertion about who determines the merit and worth of an evaluand has prompted much debate over the years. We argue in this paper that the act of valuing may be perceived in many different ways. Although Scriven and some others view valuing as lying solely in the purview of the evaluator, many other evaluation writers do not perceive the valuing act in the same way. Namely, that valuing is not just the prerogative of the evaluator. Rather than leaving the valuing act to the evaluator, some writers (e.g., Fetterman & Wandersman, 2005; Stake, 2012; Weiss, 1999) argue for the involvement of others in the valuing process and that there are many different ways in which others might be involved in the valuing process. With this being the case, we consider the ways in which valuing might take place.

Different evaluation conditions will call for different approaches to valuing. Consider the influence of context on the evaluation process. As Scriven notes in this volume, *good* and *bad* are context-dependent concepts. Thus, important dimensions of an evaluation's context include the social and political conditions under which the program is being evaluated, the issues and questions that should be addressed, and whether these questions are answerable given the evaluation's resources and constraints. Scriven describes in his writings (e.g., Scriven, this issue) how evaluative claims are established and validated.

As part of the total context in which evaluation takes place, and of particular relevance to our discussion on valuing, we consider the multiple theoretic perspectives that govern an evaluator's behavior. Each has within it an implied direction that valuing might take. We call this the *evaluator context*. At present, there are certainly various conceptions of evaluator context in the field. Some suggest that evaluators must bring to bear their methodological and interpersonal skills, content knowledge, values, and theoretic orientation when conducting evaluations (Alkin, 2012; Vo, in press). Broader definitions of the idea may include the discipline, local setting, or geographic location in which the evaluator is situated. We do not take particular issue with the appropriateness of these operationalizations here, as additional work in this area will surely lead to the development of a widely accepted definition. Rather, for the purposes of this article, we define *evaluator context* as the dispositions that may influence the way in which evaluators go about the valuing process. Specifically, this refers to the theoretic dispositions that an evaluator might have. It is the evaluator context that we are concerned with here.

Specifically, we consider how the *evaluator context* influences the valuing process and use a teaching analogy to describe the multiple approaches to valuing. Based on this analysis, we present a typology of evaluator valuing roles. This heuristic offers a more explicit understanding of the ways in which the valuing activity is framed by a theoretic lens. In general, we hope to provide a framework through which the act of valuing can be further studied.

Evaluator Contextual Influence on Valuing

By evaluator context we mean the individual evaluator's point of view, preferences, etc. Consider that there are multiple theoretic perspectives on evaluation—evaluation theories, if you will (Alkin, 2004). Alkin and Christie (2004) argue that all theorists consider valuing, along with methods and use, as part of their conceptualization about what evaluation is and how it should be conducted, regardless of whether valuing is addressed explicitly or not. Thus, each evaluation theory may carry with it implications for the way that valuing should take place within that theoretic perspective. Although theoretic approaches to evaluation may capture a portion of what we have referred to as *evaluator context*, it does not quite capture the potential variations in valuing preferences. That is, although many prescriptive theories contain clear descriptions of the various ways in which evaluation can be conducted, issues pertaining to the valuing process—who should value, with whom, to what extent, and under what conditions—are more clearly articulated by some theorists than others. We offer three broad categories for describing how valuing takes place during the evaluation process; namely, by stakeholders only, by stakeholders with the evaluator, or by the evaluator only.

Modes of Valuing

Providing go/no go–good/bad judgments is an insufficient description of the evaluator's valuing role. The evaluator's role in valuing, as it is intended based on different evaluation perspectives, is varied. We struggled with a way to characterize these differences. In doing so, we searched for a meaningful analogy that might help to better demonstrate what we have referred to as evaluator context and what helps define the valuing mode that is described and endorsed in different theoretic writings. And, we found one. We were inspired by Cronbach's depiction of evaluation as teaching (Cronbach & Associates, 1980). Cronbach maintains that the evaluator teaches so that growth in understanding will occur. Gowin and Millman (1981) describe Cronbach's point of view as: "The evaluator is an educator working so the social order learns" (p. 86). But what specifically is the process by which the evaluator acts to help members of the policy-shaping community to deepen their understandings of the program? That is not clear.

Others too have referred to evaluation as teaching. Most directly, Wise (1980), in a *New Directions for Evaluation* volume, spoke of the evaluator as educator. He noted that there are elements of evaluator as teacher in the interactions that occur. There are many others who describe one of the key roles of the evaluator as that of teacher.

Now, think for a moment about the way that teaching takes place. In formal terms, the varying approaches to teaching are categorized by Fenstermacher and Soltis (1992) as the executive approach, the facilitator approach, and the liberationist approach. As an executive, the teacher's purpose is to "acquire the specific facts, concepts, skills and ideas" (p. 4), which s/he then communicates to students. The facilitator approach depicts the teacher "as an empathetic person charged with helping individuals grow personally and reach a high level of self actualization, understanding and acceptance" (p. 4). Finally, the teacher as liberator is concerned with freeing the individual's mind for the various aligned purposes, such as "development of intellectual skills, including the skills of learning" (p. 4).

When considering different teaching processes, we envisioned similar processes for the evaluator. For instance, teachers are commonly thought of as lecturers. This is an authoritarian role, implying that the teacher is the source of knowledge, and lectures are the vehicles by which that knowledge is delivered. Another kind of teaching role is one in which the teacher engages students in discussion and guides them in reaching conclusions so that final understandings are a product of the teacher and the student.

Table 3.1. Typology of Evaluator Valuing Roles

Valuing By	Description	Exemplars
Stakeholders	Stakeholders establish standards a priori	Tyler/Popham
	Evaluator provides data to identified stakeholders	Stake
	Evaluator provides data for use by broad audiences	Cronbach/Weiss
Stakeholders and evaluator	Evaluator guides stakeholders by establishing a framework for valuing	Alkin
	Evaluator guides stakeholders by guiding the valuing process iteratively	Fetterman/Patton
	Evaluator participates with stakeholders in valuing	Cousins/King
Evaluator	Evaluator valuing strongly based on the promotion of evaluator values (e.g., morals)	House
	Evaluator valuing based upon evaluation expertise	Scriven
	Evaluator valuing based primarily on program expertise	Eisner
	Evaluator valuing based upon scientific appraisal	Boruch/Cook

Teachers may also create situations in which students learn by doing. In essence, teachers provide the context and mechanism for learning to take place. This might be done by the creation of case studies and other kinds of activities where students' learning take place through the process of engaging with materials or activities initially produced by the teacher. In this role, the teacher is the inspirational leader and social conscience of students. The learning tasks are at hand, whether in textbooks or programmed materials, and the teacher provides encouragement and attempts to instill confidence in students. Students are being equipped to take control of their own learning.

We believe that Cronbach was really onto something. We see where evaluation (and particularly "valuing" in evaluation) *is* like teaching—at least as far as providing a vehicle for recognizing the diversity of evaluation perspectives. Aided by the teaching analogy just presented, we will examine the various roles of the evaluator and present a typology of evaluator valuing roles.

Table 3.1 provides an indication of the ways that value judgments are reached by *stakeholders* alone, *stakeholders and evaluators* in consort with each other, or by the *evaluator* only. The second column provides a description of the nature of the engagement in the valuing process. Lastly, we have listed evaluation theorists whose approaches we believe exemplify the valuing processes described in the first two columns.

However, providing an indication of who is to be included in the valuing process, while important, is not enough. The question remains about the nature of that engagement. That is, what specifically are the roles of evaluators and stakeholders in the valuing process? In many ways, our three overarching valuing categories—(a) stakeholders, (b) evaluator and stakeholder, and (c) evaluator only—correspond to the teaching approaches—(a) liberationist, (b) facilitator, and (c) executive, respectively.[1]

Valuing by Stakeholders

Identified others themselves establish the standard a priori.

Evaluator provides the data but leaves the valuing to the identified primary stakeholders.

Evaluator provides the data but leaves the valuing to the general/broad others.

Let us examine each of these modes of inclusion of others in the valuing activity. First consider the situation in which "identified 'others' themselves establish the standard a priori." This instance is most clearly demonstrated when the evaluation question specified by stakeholders has within it a specific standard for judging a program's worth. Take, for example, an afterschool program where program success is indicated by a score of 75 or above on a particular assessment. Alternatively, perhaps a stipulated percent of participants achieving a specified level on a criterion-referenced test serves as the measure of program success. In these cases, the standard is either met or it is not. The valuing criterion has been well defined. An example of this kind of valuing is evident in objectives-based evaluation approaches, which focus on generating information for accountability and decision making by developing and measuring the appropriate objectives for these purposes. Tyler initially established this type of approach as an acceptable method for evaluating programs in education in his 8-year study. Later, Popham extended this approach, focusing primarily on specifying behavioral objectives. This approach to valuing relies heavily on measuring educational outcomes and as such de-emphasized the focus on the instructional process. With more precise, unambiguous objectives, it is argued that one could determine with more confidence when program outcomes have been met.

Other evaluation writers advocate for the evaluator to provide systematic data to a group of identified stakeholders so that those in this specified group can make value judgments about the evaluand. Many of those who describe the valuing process in this way are guided by a more relativist approach to evaluation. These theorists argue that the value of something changes depending upon particular circumstances, and the beliefs, values, and perspectives held by individuals. Here, it is the role of the evaluator to collect data that is contextually grounded systematically, so that stakeholders can place value on the program based on the particularities of the specific evaluand being studied. Stake, for example, argues for using a responsive evaluation, which often utilizes case studies as a method for studying the merit of an evaluand, in particular situations where a contextually grounded understanding of an evaluand is warranted. He maintains that the evaluator should offer a "thick description" of the evaluand for use by stakeholders to promote understanding of the "merit and shortcoming" of the evaluand (Stake, 2012). Stake acknowledges (personal conversation) that frequently his ideal valuing cannot be attained and he must value based on stakeholder values as he perceives them.

A third scenario where stakeholders alone place value on the evaluand is when the evaluator provides systematic data, but leaves the valuing to general/broad audiences. In this case, the evaluator is typically focused on those in the policy-making community more generally and not any one identified group of stakeholders. It is not clear when or in what specific decision-making context(s) the evaluation information might be used, and so it is the evaluator's role to offer the best systematic information possible so that when it is needed, evaluation information can be used to inform decisions. This might be seen in studies of more general issues that are of concern to federal policy makers, such as those examining early childhood development programming.

Both Cronbach and Weiss advocate for providing information for these audiences, although they describe different processes by which this information informs valuing in the policy and political contexts. Weiss argues that evaluation brings "data and generalizations based on the data into the policy system" (Weiss, 1999, p. 471). While Weiss acknowledges that this information occasionally makes a splash, much more often evaluation information slowly makes its way into the policy arena, which cumulatively and subtly influences policy. Cronbach reasons that "generalizations decay"; therefore, evaluation should be conducted to promote stronger social programming by describing program components that work under specific conditions with particular groups. This information should then inform the political community, where the "logic of science" meets "the logic of politics" (Cronbach & Associates, 1980, p. ix).

Valuing by Evaluator and Stakeholders

Evaluator provides the data and helps to establish a framework that might be used for valuing by others.
Evaluator provides the data and guides others in the valuing process iteratively.
Evaluator participates with others in the valuing act.

One way that evaluators participate with stakeholders is to act as a guide in assisting them to value. As we have noted, there is a certain amount of evaluation guidance employed in the previously discussed section on valuing by stakeholders. That is, even when the evaluator provides the data for stakeholders to make judgments based upon their own frame of reference, the evaluator—in structuring the presentation of data—is in fact participating to some extent.

One form of joint participation by the evaluator is when stakeholders (or "identified others") are guided by the evaluator in establishing a standard for judging results. Alkin (2004, 2011; Alkin, Christie, & Rose, 2006) suggests one example of this kind of inclusion, whereby the evaluator works with stakeholders a priori to develop a framework for judging results during the question identification phase of the evaluation. He suggests that evaluators "work with primary stakeholders in getting them to depict more fully the parameters of acceptability related to each question. That is, what were their views (before any data were collected), as to what would be an acceptable set of findings for each question?" (Alkin, 2004, pp. 189–190). Valuing, thus, is in large part performed by primary stakeholders before they might be biased by examining actual findings. This is done by introducing scenarios of possible findings to determine acceptability from the perspective of these stakeholders. Where qualitative instrumentation is likely to be employed, the development of a qualitative description of success might be used as a basis for a subsequent valuing comparison. This approach to valuing is well suited for evaluations guided by user-focused, context-sensitive evaluation (Alkin, 2012) frameworks.

Although not ideal, a judging framework for use by stakeholders also might be constructed following the collection of data. That is, the evaluator might at the conclusion of the data-collection process sit with stakeholders to discuss the manner in which judging could take place and even construct a valuing framework as above.

Perhaps the evaluator does not aid the stakeholders in developing a specifically defined standard for judging, but still provides guidance in valuing. We find in some of the theorists' writings, and in our conceptualization of possibilities, a position whereby evaluators provide the data and work with stakeholders in examining data and providing constructive procedural steps that might be taken in making valuing judgments. We find evidence of this level of participation in Fetterman's writings. "In empowerment evaluation, the stakeholders with assistance of the empowerment evaluators, conduct the evaluation and put the findings to use" (Fetterman & Wandersman, 2005, p. 31). This iterative assistance in guiding stakeholders is also found in Patton's work, particularly in his increasingly more salient emphasis on developmental evaluation (Patton, 2011).

But, where does "guiding" stop and "full participation" begin? We don't know but can, for the sake of argument, create this new category. We certainly see evidence of full participation by the evaluator in King's work (2005). For example, King noted in an interview conducted by Fitzpatrick that "our role [as evaluator] was facilitating" and included the "role of making sure that any claims made were proper" (Fitzpatrick, Christie, & Mark,

2009, p. 199). Cousins and Shulha (2008) also describe an evaluator valuing role in collaborative evaluations, where valuing is performed "in light of *joint* understandings of how all value positions are likely to affect the evaluation" (p. 144).

Valuing by Evaluator

Valuing strongly based on the promotion of evaluator values (e.g., morals).
Valuing based on evaluation expertise.
Valuing based on program expertise.
Valuing based upon scientific appraisal.

A bit further on this continuum is the case of the evaluator who engages in the valuing process without stakeholders' participation or input. Evaluators who value independently tend to view the task of judging an evaluand's merit or worth as their primary—and in some cases—sole responsibility. Scriven uses product evaluation to illustrate this process. Several factors shape these kinds of value judgments, including those related to the evaluator's personal values, their evaluation experience, their program expertise, and their commitment to the scientific method. Let us explore these factors in turn.

Evaluators' personal sense of what is ethical and correct shape a fair amount of the way in which many go about their practice and subsequently arrive at conclusions about what they have been charged to evaluate. These judgments are primarily based on the argument that if evaluation is indeed a value-laden activity, then it is the evaluator's fundamental responsibility to "be uncompromising about morally objectionable claims" (House & Howe, 1999, p. xxi). The striving for and attainment of social justice, in this case, are key criteria for what is considered morally correct. As such, the evaluator's role is usually cast in terms of being spokespeople of the underrepresented, powerless, and poor. Additionally, the interests and needs of these groups are weighted more heavily during the valuing process for evaluators who align themselves with this particular point of view. Evidence of this approach to valuing can be found in the works of scholars such as House, Howe, and Hopson who believe that value should inherently be defined as what is "right, fair, and just, not in terms of good or bad" (Alkin, 2004, p. 41).

Nonetheless, judgments of what is considered "good" or "bad" are possible and there exists a class of evaluators who believe that making these kinds of valuing decisions is the only activity in which evaluators should be engaged. And, because these decisions were made based not only on whether a program or product worked, but also the extent to which it was cost effective and the degree to which it produced unintended, negative effects, etc., they are the kinds of decisions that will most benefit the public. Moreover, the ability to arrive at these unbiased judgments—unbiased because stakeholders were not involved in the evaluative process and were unable to influence the evaluator's decision—calls for a different kind of appreciation for and understanding of evaluation. Most importantly, it requires evaluation expertise. The primary idea here is that everyone, rather than particular groups, will benefit from knowing what is good, bad, for whom, and under what conditions. We suggested earlier that Scriven is a strong proponent of this method of valuing and hope that we have provided adequate description for this positioning.

Yet another approach to arriving at value judgments is one that involves the ability to notice fine differences in type, quality, construction, and design. Elliot Eisner's theory of evaluation, which takes connoisseurship and criticism as its cornerstones, is an example of such an approach. Specifically, Eisner argues that to be a true connoisseur, one must have "worked at the business of learning how to see, to hear . . . to be aware of and understand the experience" (Eisner, 1991, p. 174). Eisner describes this in the context of education and art, and specifically art education. It is the extensive background knowledge—program expertise, if you will—that informs the value judgments at which evaluators arrive. However, it should be noted that this method of valuing does not apply strictly to summative judgments. Rather, it is used at every juncture in the evaluation process, including articulation and prioritization of questions, selection of data collection tools, creation of those instruments, analysis, etc.

Nonetheless, there are also evaluators who value based on their ability to explain why different social phenomena occur and how. Unlike the valuing approaches that we have previously described, value judgments of this ilk stem directly from scientifically based conclusions. Namely, appraisals that are rooted in results of a scientific study that used sound research methods. We found evidence of this kind of valuing in the works of theorists such as Robert Boruch and Thomas Cook. Boruch and Cook believe that employing randomized controlled experiments to gather valid and reliable evidence is the best route by which one can arrive at unbiased value judgments (Boruch, 1997). In this case (and presumably in cases where impact estimates are desired), judgments are considered unbiased because the process of randomization ensures a fair comparison. Although methods-based evaluators rely heavily on the scientific process to inform their final decision about merit and worth, that is not to say that they do not value stakeholder input en route to that decision. Boruch (2004), for example, has indicated that, "[Stakeholders] are partners . . . whose cooperation is necessary in the trials. Investing in these people, when they can be trusted and can trust the evaluator, is part of better understanding what leads to better trials" (p. 120). In this case, the stakeholder's role is to inform the evaluator of what questions they would like addressed, but it is the evaluator's responsibility to determine how best to answer those questions, and the answers are grounded in research methods. The evaluator, as the analyst and interpreter of research findings, communicates with stakeholders about what has been learned. Therefore, the valuing act rests with the evaluator.

We have explored valuing based on the use of quantitative methods. However, we were also troubled by whether there is a theorist who makes value judgments based strictly on qualitative or descriptive methods. To some extent, Eisner is heavily dependent on qualitative methods, but perhaps not solely dependent on those judgments. We thought about Jennifer Greene, who employs mixed methods, but we are not entirely convinced that she is not oriented toward participating with stakeholders. Perhaps she provides them data so that they can form their own value judgments, but we leave that as an open question.

In Summary

Have we placed theorists properly? In examining evaluator context, we placed theorists as exemplars for certain categories. This was a difficult task and we can well imagine many of our colleagues bemoaning their improper placement. We understand some of the potential concerns with this exercise, but in our defense, note that absent from many theorists' writings are detailed descriptions the specific role the evaluator (and others) have in the valuing act. As indicated, the evaluator still intercedes in some manner even for those theorists who argue that stakeholders should have a key role in the valuing process. So clearly substantial overlap exists and certainly, the larger evaluation context, which we do not address in this paper, has an influence on the evaluator context as we describe it.

Final Comment

Conclusion: the evaluator engages in a process, a major element of which is assuring that valuing will occur. We must recognize the diversity of contexts, both evaluation context and evaluator context, and not insist that all evaluators perform valuing in one (presumed) "right" way.

It is clear to us that there is no singular way of portraying the role of the evaluator in valuing. There are a variety of evaluator approaches and each carries with it different implications for the way that valuing transpires. Evaluators can be engaged in valuing by guiding stakeholders in the process of reaching conclusions about value. Evaluators can be engaged in valuing by acting as a social conscience in reflecting on the meaning of findings. Evaluators can assist in valuing by providing stakeholders with the opportunity to actively engage in evaluation and, in that process, themselves determine the worth of an enterprise. And yes, evaluators can perceive their role as personally making a decision of merit or worth.

Based on what we have now seen, let us expand on Scriven's definition of valuing and redefine the role of the evaluator in valuing. It is our view that the role of the evaluator in valuing is to activate, facilitate a structure, be engaged in, and contribute to the process of determining merit or worth.

Moreover, attention to different program contexts may lead evaluation theorists to modify their mode of valuing based upon the demands of the particular context. As a result, an evaluator is never solely in one category. It is also likely, though, that evaluators choose to work in evaluation contexts in which their approach can be best implemented and will be most useful. What we have attempted to do is to portray theorists in what we believe to be their most prevalent mode based on our understanding of their writings.

Note

1. There are indeed other implications of these teaching approaches that can help illuminate discussions on evaluation theory and practice. To address this would be beyond the scope of this article. See Christie and Alkin (2012) for a more in-depth discussion of the relationships among the key dimensions of evaluation theory and practice, methods, valuing, and use.

References

Alkin, M. C. (Ed.). (2004). *Evaluation roots: Tracing theorists' views and influences.* Thousand Oaks, CA: Sage.

Alkin, M. C. (2011). *Evaluation essentials: From A to Z.* New York, NY: Guilford Press.

Alkin, M. C. (2012). Context sensitive evaluation. In M. C. Alkin (Ed.), *Evaluation roots: A wider perspective of theorists' views and influences* (2nd ed.). Thousand Oaks, CA: Sage.

Alkin, M. C., & Christie, C. A. (2004). An evaluation theory tree. In M. C. Alkin (Ed.), *Evaluation roots: Tracing theorists' views and influences* (pp. 12–66). Thousand Oaks, CA: Sage.

Alkin, M. C., Christie, C. A., & Rose, M. (2006). Communicating evaluation. In I. Shaw, J. Greene, & M. Marks (Eds.), *Sage handbook of evaluation* (pp. 384–403). Thousand Oaks, CA: Sage.

Boruch, R. (1997). *Randomized experiments for planning and evaluation.* Thousand Oaks, CA: Sage.

Boruch, R. (2004). A trialist's notes on evaluation theory and roots. In M. C. Alkin (Ed.), *Evaluation roots: Tracing theorists' views and influences* (pp. 114–121). Thousand Oaks, CA: Sage.

Christie, C. A., & Alkin, M. C. (2012). An evaluation theory tree. In M. C. Alkin (Ed.), *Evaluation roots: A wider perspective of theorists' views and influences* (2nd ed.). Thousand Oaks, CA: Sage.

Cousins, J. B., & Shulha, L. M. (2008). Complexities in setting program standards. In N. Smith & P. Brandon (Eds.), *Fundamental issues in evaluation* (pp. 139–158). New York, NY: Guilford Press.

Cronbach, L. J., & Associates. (1980). *Toward reform of program evaluation.* San Francisco, CA: Jossey-Bass.

Eisner, E. (1991). Taking a second look: Educational connoisseurship revisited. In M. W. McLaughlin & D. C. Phillips (Eds.), *Evaluation and education: At quarter century* (90th yearbook of the National Society for the Study of Education, Part II, pp. 169–187). Chicago, IL: University of Chicago Press.

Fenstermacher, G. D., & Soltis, J. F. (1992). *Approaches to teaching.* New York, NY: Teachers College Press.

Fetterman, D., & Wandersman, A. (2005). *Empowerment principles in practice.* New York, NY: Guilford Press.

Fitzpatrick, J., Christie, C. A., & Mark, M. (2009). *Evaluation in action: Interviews with evaluators.* Thousand Oaks, CA: Sage.

Fournier, D. (2005). Evaluation. In S. Mathison (Ed.), *Encyclopedia of evaluation* (pp. 139–140). Thousand Oaks, CA: Sage.

Gowin, B., & Millman, J. (1981). Book review: Toward reform of program evaluation: Lee J. Cronbach, S. R. Ambron, S. M. Dornbusch, R. D. Hess, R. C. Hornik, D. C. Phillips, D. F. Walker, & S. S. Weiner. *Educational Evaluation and Policy Analysis, 3*(6), 85–87.

House, E., & Howe, K. (1999). *Values in evaluation and social research.* Thousand Oaks, CA: Sage.

King, J. (2005). A proposal to build evaluation capacity at the Bunche–Da Vinci Learning Partnership Academy. *New Directions for Evaluation, 106,* 85–98.

Patton, M. Q. (2011). *Developmental evaluation: Applying complexity concepts to enhance innovation and use.* New York, NY: Guilford Press.

Scriven, M. (1986). New frontiers of evaluation. *Evaluation Practice, 7*(1), 7–44.

Scriven, M. (2003). Evaluation theory and metatheory. In T. Kellaghan & D. Stufflebeam (Eds.), *International Handbook of Educational Evaluation* (pp. 15–30). Boston, MA: Kluwer.

Scriven, M. (2012). Conceptual revolutions in evaluation. In M. C. Alkin (Ed.), *Evaluation roots: A wider perspective of theorists' views and influences* (2nd ed.). Thousand Oaks, CA: Sage.

Stake, R. (2012). Responsive evaluation IV. In M. C. Alkin (Ed.), *Evaluation roots: A wider perspective of theorists' views and influences* (2nd ed.). Thousand Oaks, CA: Sage.

Vo, A. T. (in press). Visualizing context through theory decomposition. *Evaluation and Program Planning.*

Weiss, C. (1999). The interface between evaluation and public policy. *Evaluation, 5,* 468–486.

Wise, R. I. (1980). The evaluator as educator. *New Directions for Program Evaluation, 5,* 11–18.

MARVIN C. ALKIN is a professor emeritus in the Social Research Methodology Division of the Graduate School of Education and Information Studies at the University of California, Los Angeles.

ANNE T. VO is a doctoral candidate in the Social Research Methodology Division of the Graduate School of Education and Information Studies at the University of California, Los Angeles, and a coeditor of the teaching evaluation section in the American Journal of Evaluation.

CHRISTINA A. CHRISTIE is associate professor in the Social Research Methodology Division of the Graduate School of Education and Information Studies at the University of California, Los Angeles.

Yates, B. T. (2012). Step arounds for common pitfalls when valuing resources used versus resources produced. In G. Julnes (Ed.), *Promoting valuation in the public interest: Informing policies for judging value in evaluation. New Directions for Evaluation, 133,* 43–52.

4

Step Arounds for Common Pitfalls When Valuing Resources Used Versus Resources Produced

Brian T. Yates

Abstract

The value of a program can be understood as referring not only to outcomes, but also to how those outcomes compare to the types and amounts of resources expended to produce the outcomes. Major potential mistakes and biases in assessing the worth of resources consumed, as well as the value of outcomes produced, are explored. Most of these occur when the evaluation is limited in contexts examined or perspectives adopted. In particular, it is noted that the price of a resource often is context-dependent, and may not describe the value of a resource from important perspectives. Also, the monetary value of outcomes as inferred from earned income, and from avoided human service expenditures, may not reflect outcome value from key perspectives, possibly exacerbating discrimination according to gender, ethnicity, and age. Solutions for these problems are recommended. More complete and detailed information on resources consumed and outcomes produced also may facilitate systematic optimization of program value, if the evaluation includes the amounts and types of resources used by those program activities that change the participant processes that lead to desired program outcomes. © Wiley Periodicals, Inc., and the American Evaluation Association.

The cynic . . . knows the price of everything and the value of nothing.
—Oscar Wilde's *Lady Windermere's Fan*

NEW DIRECTIONS FOR EVALUATION, no. 133, Spring 2012 © Wiley Periodicals, Inc., and the American Evaluation Association. Published online in Wiley Online Library (wileyonlinelibrary.com) • DOI: 10.1002/ev.20005

Evaluators rarely are cynics . . . at least at the start of an evaluation. Also of note about evaluators is that they rarely consider the types and amounts of resources consumed by a program when evaluating it. Instead, the activities of the program and the reactions of participants and onlookers to those activities often are the primary focus. Even evaluations that appear to include costs typically report only the summed current value of resources purchased for use in the program, that is, the total price paid, which often conveys less information than is needed to describe programs accurately and to optimize programs systematically.

For example, how students react emotionally to the educational process in which they have participated is captured qualitatively and measured quantitatively in many evaluations of teaching. Changes in students' knowledge of facts and theories, and students' performance of skills from computations to therapies, also are assessed in some of evaluations of teaching. Even the amount of money spent per student may be reported. But does any of this help us judge the *value* of the education that was received? Not really. Furthermore, does this evaluation of teaching help us understand what actually happened, why some goals were achieved and others were not, and most importantly how to *improve* the education? Again, no.

Knowing the summary price at which a service was purchased does not establish the value of the service, especially when that service is not available in a free market and purchasable by a large number of rational decision-makers (as is common in many programs). Instead, we can begin the valuing process of most human services by asking what made the service possible. For teaching, that would be the training, time, and effort of the teachers, most likely. Anything else? Perhaps the time spent or not spent by students and possibly their parents or tutors in educational activities, plus the knowledge and skills students already have or have not acquired, could contribute to or detract from education outcomes. Are any other resources used in a program of education? Brick-and-mortar buildings, possibly . . . and some form of information technology, certainly, whether texts or computers, probably supported by administrative and other services.

These resources that make possible program operations and outcomes are ignored entirely or mentioned tangentially in most evaluations, despite decades of efforts to persuade evaluators to include costs in evaluations of education, mental health, substance-abuse treatment, and other programs (e.g., Carter & Newman, 1976; Fishman, 1975; Levine & McEwan, 2001; Sorensen & Phipps, 1975; Yates, 1980, 1996). Many evaluations compare outcomes of these programs. Most evaluators probably recognize that different amounts or types of resources could produce different outcomes for the programs they evaluate . . . yet exceptionally few evaluators and evaluations report or compare costs!

Ignoring the *contextual pragmatics* of those resources available to, and used by, a program risks making attributions about the potential effectiveness of programs that may be more accurately attributed to the resources that were or were not available at the sites at which the program was implemented. Consider, for instance, the inaccuracy as well as the inequity of comparing educational outcomes at well- and poorly funded schools (cf. Ross, Barkaoui, & Scott, 2007). Blaming relatively poor student performance on the educational methods, teachers, principals, or students could be incorrect, and could lead to harmful personnel and funding decisions, if the school had been underfunded relative to other schools. Yet most evaluations exclude meaningful information on the types and amounts of resources that were and were not available to the program in the context in which it operated during the evaluation. Particularly in times of increasing constraints on many resources needed by human services, program evaluations seem incomplete and even impractical unless they include the resources available to and used by programs in the contexts in which they try to operate. Particularly because outcomes are distal and probabilistic while resource expenditures are more proximal and certain, including in an evaluation information about the resources consumed by a program seems at least as important as information about outcomes attained by a program.

Step Arounds for Pitfalls and Biases in Evaluating Resources Consumed by Programs

Evaluating program costs involves more than simply listing *prices* paid at a particular time and place to acquire the resources used by the program. The money one had to pay to obtain these resources can be a poor representation of their worth, as Mr. Wilde noted at the start of this manuscript. Price is a function of contextual features such as demand by other programs and availability, and can be manipulated to create artificial scarcity or exaggerate apparent abundance. Rather, a cost-inclusive evaluation can better help a program achieve its goals by including a description of the types and amounts of specific resources used by a program, plus the specific activities that those resources were used to enable (cf. Yates, 1996). This information allows managers to adjust the degree to which different program activities are implemented in response to changes in the resources available (cf. Yates, 1980).

Substantial errors in managing, understanding, and disseminating programs in different contexts can be introduced if an evaluation provides an incomplete description of resources used by a program at particular sites. These incomplete resource valuations are more common in mono-perspective evaluations, in addition to other problems described by Alkin, Vo, and Christie (this issue). Too often, evaluations that attempt to incorporate costs ignore resources contributed by program participants, such as time spent by clients when receiving program services. This *nonvaluing* of participant time can be interpreted as profoundly *devaluing* the client, a bias that can lead to excessive reliance on resources that are scarce for many clients. Client time spent receiving services has intrinsic value, to clients and client advocates at least. Client time may have no monetary value or "price" according to some stakeholders, in that the client may not be employable or may not work outside the home. The cost to family members of replacing some clients' time in the home can be considerable,however, if childcare or housework was being provided by the client prior to inpatiency. Similarly, unless the client resides in the program facility, time and expense traveling to and from program sites is an additional resource seldom included in program evaluations. Excluding these and other client resource expenditures not only provides an incomplete depiction of the program, but also underestimates the value of total resources consumed by the program.

Moreover, clients of most human services are asked to seek services in addition to those of the program being evaluated, such as vocational training or support groups. Client time, client funds, and client transportation spent because of these referrals, and the resources consumed by the referred-to services when actually used, can be critical to include. Otherwise an evaluation might erroneously report substantial returns for minimal investments that actually required more resources of society because of unreported use of other programs' services.

In addition, time spent by service providers may be underrepresented by time recorded in payroll records. In primary and second school, for example, teachers may spent entire evenings beyond their recognized working hours grading and commenting on assignments and tests. In mental health services, too, some providers receive little or no money, volunteering substantial time and costly transportation resources in exchange for supervision and training at externships and internships required for graduate degrees and licensure (e.g., Yates, Haven, & Thoresen, 1979).

Resources other than provider and client time may be consumed but not reported accurately or at all in budgets. These include donated facilities, equipment and materials donated, and administrative services and utilities paid for by a parent organization but omitted from the evaluation report (e.g., Yates et al., 2011). In sum, a full accounting of resources used by a program describes what the program uses and consumes. Accounting records alone can underrepresent those resources in ways that can distort evaluation findings.

Evaluating Program Value as What Is Produced Relative to What Is Consumed

When judging the value of a program in the context of constrained funding, outcomes are meaningless until they are compared to the types and amounts of resources consumed to produce them.

—Anonymous

NEW DIRECTIONS FOR EVALUATION • DOI: 10.1002/ev

Where does such a bold statement come from? From the perspective of many decision makers who use evaluations! For funders, programs are means of transforming those resources that are available in a community into something the funder is responsible to foster or maintain—turning uneducated children into educated adults, for example. Moreover, in light of the diminishing availability of many resources for most needs, funders also weigh not only whether more resources were produced than were consumed by individual programs, but how the net benefit of some programs compares to the net benefit of other, alternative programs. For many programs, including substance-abuse treatment and psychological services, benefits such as increased licit income and reduced use of health, mental health, and criminal justice services are 9.7 to 14.9 times larger than the costs of those programs—see, for example, French et al. (2000).

So, is this what *value*-ation of a program has come to: comparison of the resources used (costs) versus the outcomes produced (benefits)? Yes. Must we evaluators really consider doing cost–benefit analysis now? Could not this attention to program costs, benefits, and net benefit be delegated to other professionals, or postponed until we have thoroughly evaluated the outcomes of a program?

Yes, indeed. We evaluators do not have to evaluate costs and benefits and compare the two. Others will, and increasingly are. *Their* findings are the ones that will decide which programs receive public monies and which will not. In contrast to the tentative approaches of the legislatures of the United States (Shipman, this issue) and Canada (Dumaine, this issue), some state legislatures have been using available cost–benefit analyses to decide which programs to fund. Building on initial findings from the turn of the century, for example, the Washington State legislature in 2009 directed its policy institute to: ". . . calculate the return on investment to taxpayers from evidence-based prevention and intervention programs and policies." The legislature instructed the institute to produce "a comprehensive list of programs and policies that improve . . . outcomes for children and adults in Washington and result in more cost-efficient use of public resources" (Aos et al., 2011, p. 1).

The results of funding only those programs that showed the highest return on investment of taxpayer funds already have convinced the Washington state legislature to continue making funding decisions according to findings of evaluations that include monetary benefits as well as costs:

> Today, the results of these crime-focused efforts appear to be paying off. Relative to national rates, juvenile crime has dropped in Washington, adult criminal recidivism has declined, total crime is down, and taxpayer criminal justice costs are lower than alternative strategies would have required. (Aos et al., 2011, page 1)

My advice: we evaluators should abandon our apparent *value phobia* (Scriven, this issue) with regard to cost–benefit relationships as well as valuation more generally. We should embrace and report multiperspective valuations of those resources that make possible the specific activities that lead to targeted program outcomes.

Step Arounds for Pitfalls and Biases in Evaluating Resources *Produced* by Programs

To minimize exaggeration of program benefits relative to program costs, resources produced by a program need to be evaluated at least as thoroughly and carefully as the resources consumed by the program (cf. Glick, Doshi, Sonnad, & Polsky, 2007; Gold, Siegel, Russell, & Weinstein, 1996). However, just as boiling down information on diverse resources consumed by a program into a single "price" can hide omission of resources critical to understanding and establishing a similar program in another setting, so can reducing the many outcomes of a program into a single monetary figure exclude information essential to an accurate understanding of what a program accomplishes. One common outcome measured in evaluations of resources generated by programs is hoped-for increments in client income. Another outcome commonly measured in benefit valuations is savings that can result from participation in program activities, such as when substance-abuse treatment reduces subsequent use of health and criminal justice services (e.g., Mannix, 2010). Both income enhancement and service savings typically are valued in local currency units, such as additional dollars earned and dollars saved. Often these are summed to form a measure of the *benefits* of the program. Distilling these resource-related outcomes into a single number can hide errors in valuation.

For example, clients whose incomes differ not according to productivity but according to gender, age, ethnicity, or country may appear to benefit to different extents from the same program. A program that put back to work a 35-year-old male could appear, for instance, to be more beneficial in future annual income earned than a program that returned to work a 35-year-old female, due to ignominious disparities in pay for males versus females. Also, in terms of projected total earnings over one's lifetime, a program that returned to work a 35-year-old female could appear more beneficial than one that returned to work a 65-year-old male, because of the likely longer remaining lifetimes of the female versus the male. Furthermore, a substance-abuse treatment program that reduces health care utilization for males might appear less beneficial than a substance-abuse treatment program that reduces the higher levels of health care utilization found for most females, even though the same proportional reduction in service utilization was produced for both genders (cf. Mannix, 2010). Finally, treatment and prevention of a disease that diminishes productivity could be viewed as more beneficial for countries in which residents had higher earning potential.

NEW DIRECTIONS FOR EVALUATION • DOI: 10.1002/ev

One possible solution to these problems is to accept the observed or projected differences in income and service savings as valid indicators of differential program benefits. It has been argued that this practice could lead to funding decisions for employment programs that perpetuate or exacerbate current social inequities for women versus men, for different ethnicities, and for the aging (Yates, 1986). A preferable alternative may be to use pay rates that are standardized across genders, ethnicities, ages, countries, and other variables on which differences in income and health care use exist. Also, constants reflecting the complete value of a health service could be used to monetize future expenditures for those more accurately, rather than using the rates set for publicly funded services, such as Medicaid and Medicare. The latter could underestimate the benefits of services, such as substance abuse treatment, that reduce future health care expenditures.

Conducting evaluations in ways that consider these potential problems in measuring program outcomes could provide more socially valid assessments of program value, as called for by Morris (this issue). An alternative approach to attempting to monetize program outcomes is to find a unit of outcome measurement that can be combined with measures of program resources while being sufficiently general to allow comparison of a variety of programs. One promising measure is the quality-adjusted life year or QALY (cf. Drummond, Sculpher, Torrance, O'Brien, & Stoddard, 2005; Gold et al., 1996; e.g., Freed, Rohan, & Yates, 2007). QALYs have been standardized for a variety of medical and psychological treatments via surveys that ask individuals to judge what proportion of a year of complete health would be equivalent to a full year of life with a particular malady. Combining this information with findings on program effectiveness allows expression of a health improvement as a portion of a QALY gained due to the program. The relative value of programs then can be compared in terms of QALYs gained. The societal value of these programs is assessed by including findings on the value of the resources that were consumed to cause the increment in QALYs, as in "cost per quality-adjusted life year gained." This also is one major way to include measures of outcomes that, as Morris (this issue) notes, are more important to some interest groups than increments in productivity and decrements in future spending for other services.

The Biggest Step Around: Evaluate *More* Than Resources Consumed and Resources Produced

Questions about the value of a program can stop at the summative, "Does the program generate more, or fewer, resources than it consumes?" or the comparative summative, "Does the program produce more resources relative to those it consumes than is the case for other programs?" These are important questions that, when answered in ways that avoid the pitfalls explored above, can help decision makers better allocate societal resources for the collective good. If evaluation has a more *formative* function, however (Chelimsky, 1997; Scriven, 1967), it may be helpful to understand what did and did not occur between the consumption of resources and the hoped-for generation and savings of resources. This understanding is aided, and may only be possible, if the evaluation includes information on the types and amounts of activities in which participants engage. Even this third type of information may not be enough. If the typical causal chain of events is hypothesized, a complete theory or model of a program would include:

- Resources consumed by the program
- Activities made possible by those resources, and that the program used to engage participants
- Processes that occurred inside the brains and bodies of participants as a result of program activities
- Outcomes that were observed as a result of those processes (Yates, 1996)

This resource–activity–process–outcome (RAPO) framework can help evaluators model and understand how a program produces its outcomes. This sort of more complete model also can help an evaluator understand why a program yielded outcomes that were the opposite of those it was designed and funded to achieve, for example, increased rather than decreased use of alcohol, tobacco, and other drugs. For instance, RAPO analysis of a drug-use prevention program indicated that program activities that consumed the fewest resources per student (small student groups, which used little teacher and parent time, and little classroom space) actually decreased rather than increased social responsibility in fourth-grade students (cf. Yates, 2002). This decreased social responsibility, was, in turn, associated with higher use of alcohol, tobacco, and other drugs. If individual student participation in each of the specific activities of this substance-use prevention program had not been measured, and several psychosocial processes (including social responsibility) had not been assessed as well, the specific iatrogenic component of the program might not have been identified in the evaluation.

An additional advantage of including activities and processes as well as resources and outcomes in an evaluation is the possibility that these four variables could be combined into a quantitative model of the program. Such a model can be manipulated to find ways to optimize relationships between resources used and outcomes achieved by the program (Yates, 1996). After entering resource, activity, process, and outcome data, the model manipulation technique *linear programming* finds the combination of activities that should maximize program outcomes within the specific resource constraints of the program context (Yates, 1980). Similar analyses could find the mixture of activities that should minimize the costs of achieving specific outcomes. Maximization of benefits given available resources, and minimization of resources consumed to achieve set benefits, are especially compelling visions of how program value might not only be evaluated, but optimized.

New Directions for Evaluation • DOI: 10.1002/ev

Conclusions

1. Evaluations that exclude information on the types and amounts of resources available and used by programs may arrive at erroneous conclusions that could lead to harmful funding decisions.
2. Prices paid for resources used by programs may not provide accurate, useful descriptions of those resources.
3. Valuing resources used by programs from multiple perspectives, such as those of clients and providers, can provide more complete and accurate, and less biased, cost assessment.
4. Multiple perspectives, such as those of clients, decision makers, and taxpayers, also can describe and value the types and amounts of resources *produced* by programs in a more accurate and less biased manner.
5. Program outcomes need not be measured as money produced or saved, even when comparing those outcomes to program costs. Outcomes of diverse human services can be expressed as QALY outcomes, for example, and can be compared in terms of resources consumed to produce those QALYs.
6. Program value can be optimized if the evaluation includes information on activities and resulting changes in client processes that contribute to program outcomes, in addition to the resources used and outcomes yielded.
7. Given the above points, comparison of program outcomes generated to program resources used, or cost–benefit analysis, need not be a narrow lens on program performance. Multiperspective RAPO analyses can provide a comprehensive, formative, and influential means of providing the best services to the most people for the least amount of resources.

References

Aos, S., Lee, S., Drake, E., Pennucci, A., Klima, T., Miller, M., . . . & Burley, M. (2011). *Return on investment: Evidence-based options to improve statewide outcomes* (Document No. 11–07–1201). Olympia, WA: Washington State Institute for Public Policy.

Carter, D. E., & Newman, F. L. (1976). *A client-oriented system of mental health service delivery and program management: A workbook and guide* (pp. 76–307). Rockville, MD: Department of Health, Education, & Welfare.

Chelimsky, E. (1997). The coming transformation in evaluation. In E. Chelimsky & W. R. Shadish (Eds.), *Evaluation for the 21st century: A handbook*. Thousand Oaks, CA: Sage.

Drummond, M. F., Sculpher, M. J., Torrance, G. W., O'Brien, B. J., & Stoddard, G. L. (2005). *Methods for economic evaluation of health care programs*. Oxford: Oxford University Press.

Fishman, D. B. (1975). Development of a generic cost-effectiveness methodology for evaluating patient services of a community mental health center. In J. Zusman & C. R. Wurster (Eds.), *Program evaluation: Alcohol, drug abuse, and mental health services*. Lexington, MA: Lexington Books.

Freed, M. C., Rohan, K. J., & Yates, B. T. (2007). Estimating health utilities and quality adjusted life years in seasonal affective disorder research. *Journal of Affective Disorders, 100,* 83–89.

French, M. T., Salomé, H. J., Krupski, A., McKay, J. R., Donovan, D. M., Mclellan, A. T., & Durell, J. (2000). Benefit–cost analysis of residential and outpatient addiction treatment in the State of Washington. *Evaluation Review, 24,* 609–634. DOI: 10.1177/0193841X0002400603

Glick, H. A., Doshi, J. A., Sonnad, S. S., & Polsky, D. (2007). *Economic evaluation in clinical trials.* London: Oxford University Press.

Gold, M. R., Siegel, J. E., Russell, L. B., & Weinstein, M. C. (Eds.). (1996). *Cost-effectiveness in health and medicine.* New York: Oxford University Press.

Levine, H. M., & McEwan, P. J. (2001). *Cost-effectiveness analysis* (2nd ed.). Thousand Oaks, CA: Sage.

Mannix, D. (2010). *Gender differences in the costs, benefits, cost-effectiveness, and cost-benefit of substance abuse treatment: A study in four treatment settings* (Unpublished doctoral dissertation). Department of Psychology, American University, Washington, DC.

Ross, J. A., Barkaoui, K., & Scott, G. (2007). Evaluations that consider the cost of educational programs: The contribution of high-quality studies. *American Journal of Evaluation, 28,* 477–492.

Scriven, M. (1967). The methodology of evaluation. In R. W. Tyler, R. M. Gagne, & M. Scriven (Eds.), *Perspectives of curriculum evaluation.* Chicago, IL: Rand-McNally.

Sorensen, J. E., & Phipps, D. W. (1975). *Cost-finding and rate-setting for community mental health centers.* Rockville, MD: Department of Health, Education, & Welfare.

Yates, B. T. (1980). *Improving effectiveness and reducing costs in mental health.* Springfield, IL: Thomas.

Yates, B. T. (1986). Economics of suicide: Toward cost-effectiveness and cost-benefit analysis of suicide prevention. In R. Cross (Ed.), *Non-natural death: Coming to terms with suicide, euthanasia, withholding or withdrawing treatment.* Denver, CO: Rose Medical Center.

Yates, B. T. (1996). *Analyzing costs, procedures, processes, and outcomes in human services: An introduction.* Thousand Oaks, CA: Sage Publications.

Yates, B. T. (2002). Roles for psychological procedures, and psychological processes, in cost-offset research: Cost → procedure → process → outcome analysis. In N. A. Cummings, W. T. O'Donohue, & K. E. Ferguson (Eds.), *The impact of medical cost offset on practice and research: Making it work for you* (pp. 91–123). Reno, NV: Context Press.

Yates, B. T., Haven, W. G., & Thoresen, C. E. (1979). Cost-effectiveness analysis at Learning House: How much change for how much money? In J. S. Stumphauzer (Ed.), *Progress in behavior therapy with delinquents* (pp. 186–222). Springfield, IL: Charles C. Thomas.

Yates, B. T., Mannix, D., Freed, M. C., Campbell, J., Johnsen, M., Jones, K., & Blyler, C. (2011). Consumer-operated service programs: Monetary and donated costs and cost-effectiveness. *Psychiatric Rehabilitation Journal, 35*(2), 91–99.

BRIAN T. YATES is a professor in the Department of Psychology at the American University in Washington, DC, where he teaches, conducts research on program evaluation, and directs the Program Evaluation Research Lab (PERL). Most of his publications apply cost-effectiveness or cost-benefit analysis to the systematic evaluation and improvement of human services.

Shipman, S. (2012). The role of context in valuing federal programs. In G. Julnes (Ed.), *Promoting valuation in the public interest: Informing policies for judging value in evaluation. New Directions for Evaluation, 133*, 53–63.

5

The Role of Context in Valuing Federal Programs

Stephanie Shipman

Abstract

The author uses her experience at the U.S. Government Accountability Office (GAO), one of Congress's primary sources of evaluative information on federal programs, to provide some insight into issues involved in deciding how to evaluate a federal program or policy. She asserts that although policy makers may look to evaluations for advice on which programs work and which do not in order to make evidence-based budget decisions, most federal program evaluations simply identify program strengths and weaknesses and do not provide overall assessments or funding recommendations. How valuing is done in federally sponsored evaluations, therefore, depends on a range of contextual factors discussed in the chapter. © Wiley Periodicals, Inc., and the American Evaluation Association.

The nature of federal policy making—forging compromise among the interests of multiple stakeholders—means evaluation of federal programs must recognize the diverse interests of those stakeholders to provide credible useful information for effective management and oversight. Although some define evaluation as the assessment of a program's worth or

---

The opinions expressed are those of the author and do not represent the opinions or policies of the U.S. Government Accountability Office.

NEW DIRECTIONS FOR EVALUATION, no. 133, Spring 2012 © Wiley Periodicals, Inc., and the American Evaluation Association. Published online in Wiley Online Library (wileyonlinelibrary.com) • DOI: 10.1002/ev.20006

value, an evaluator must be very cautious about attempting to draw overall conclusions about a program's value in an environment of multiple stakeholders and evaluation purposes. And, although policy makers may look to evaluations for advice on which programs work and which do not in order to make evidence-based budget decisions, most federal program evaluations simply identify program strengths and weaknesses and do not provide overall assessments or funding recommendations. How valuing is done in federally sponsored evaluations, therefore, depends on a range of contextual factors. My experience at the U.S. Government Accountability Office (GAO), one of Congress's primary sources of evaluative information on federal programs, may provide some insight into issues involved in deciding how to evaluate a federal program or policy.

GAO's Role in Supporting Oversight of Federal Programs

GAO is an investigative agency in the legislative branch of the federal government whose mission is to support the Congress in carrying out its constitutional responsibilities and to help improve the performance and ensure the accountability of the federal government for the benefit of the American people. To fulfill that mission, GAO conducts a wide range of audits, evaluations, investigations, and other analyses, producing over 1,000 reports and 200 congressional testimonies a year. To address issues spanning the entire federal government, GAO employs a wide range of professional staff—social scientists, accountants, economists, public policy analysts, attorneys, computer experts, and specialists in fields ranging from foreign policy to health care.

GAO work is quite varied and most (about 90%) is done at the request of congressional committees or mandated by law. GAO supports congressional oversight by

- Auditing agency operations to determine whether funds are being spent efficiently and effectively
- Reporting on how well government programs and policies are meeting their objectives
- Investigating allegations of improper or illegal activities
- Performing policy analyses and outlining options for congressional consideration
- Issuing legal decisions and opinions, such as bid-protest rulings and reports on agency rules

However, only the first two activities would be typically considered program evaluations, that is, systematic assessments of the manner and extent to which a program is meeting its intended objectives.

Given its unusually broad range of work, GAO has no single approach to conducting studies or valuing federal programs, but instead develops an approach for each study appropriate to the specific request and circumstances. As an audit agency whose mission is to support the elected legislature's decision making, GAO strives to be fact based, objective, nonpartisan, nonideological, fair, and balanced in its analyses. This is critical because the audience for GAO reports is not just the requesting committee, but all the parties involved in making decisions based on that information—the Congress, the President and federal agencies, and the American public.

Of course, GAO is not the only organization conducting evaluations of federal programs and policies. Federal agencies conduct (or commission) many studies and assessments, as do the independent agency Inspectors General, the National Academies of Sciences, and various non-governmental research organizations. The Inspectors General generally focus on conducting audits and investigations of agency operations, and some evaluate how well programs are meeting their objectives. The National Academies conduct comprehensive program reviews and policy analyses at the request of Congress, typically, through review of existing evidence. Another legislative branch support agency, the Congressional Research Service, and the executive branch's Office of Management and Budget (OMB) conduct reviews of federal programs and policies, primarily through the analysis of existing data and studies. In addition, the Congressional Budget Office analyzes the spending and revenue effects of the President's budget proposals and specific legislative proposals.

Range of GAO Evaluation Questions and Approaches

Congressional requests for GAO program evaluations pose a range of questions concerning whether agency funds are being spent efficiently and effectively, and how well programs and policies are meeting their objectives. These requests are addressed with what might be best characterized as management reviews and program implementation and effectiveness evaluations.

Management reviews address whether an agency has internal control procedures in place to safeguard government resources from waste, fraud and abuse, and the financial management, human capital, and information technology systems to ensure that agencies have the appropriate resources to carry out their missions efficiently and effectively. These reviews may be broad—addressing the operation of multiple systems—or narrow—assessing the availability of critical foreign language skills, for example. Management reviews typically involve assessing the compliance of agency procedures with specific laws, regulations, and official policies, or adherence to recognized standards.

Program implementation evaluations address questions about compliance of program activities with law and regulation and conformance to other program expectations, and may address issues of service quality, operational efficiency, or obstacles to progress. Examples include whether an agency set and followed clear and objective guidelines for assessing grant applications or was successful in streamlining grantee reporting requirements.

Questions about program effectiveness may address the extent to which the program reached its target audience, achieved desired outcomes, or whether it resulted in unintended outcomes. Examples include reviewing an agency's efforts to identify and disseminate information on effective program approaches or assessing the effectiveness of community-revitalization tax expenditures. Drawing conclusions about program effectiveness, of course, usually requires carefully designed studies to isolate the program's contributions from other influences on outcomes. Because GAO lacks control over how a program operates, experimental designs are not generally employed. Instead, GAO often addresses effectiveness questions through analysis of existing data and synthesis of previous evaluations. Indeed, a large part of GAO's work consists of providing thorough, objective assessments of the credible evidence available on program effects, assessments that often conclude that the evidence is insufficient to draw conclusions on program effectiveness.

Evaluation Conclusions Depend on Available Criteria

GAO analysts do not impose their own values in making program or policy assessments, but select criteria they believe will be considered objective and appropriate for answering the study question by readers of the report. After all, the credibility and usefulness of a study's conclusions and recommendations are largely dependent on the credibility of the criteria and evidence used to draw those conclusions. Many congressional requests pose descriptive questions about an agency's activities or the size of the problem, and thus do not involve evaluative criteria or conclusions. But, where GAO is asked to draw an evaluative conclusion about how well an agency has performed or a program has achieved its goals, GAO must identify appropriate criteria and evidence with which to assess agency or program performance objectively.

Sources of Evaluative Criteria

As Scriven (this issue) notes, evaluation criteria specify the required or desired state or expectation regarding the program or operations being evaluated. To support objective assessment, criteria must be directly observable and measurable events, actions, or characteristics that provide evidence that those expectations have been met. The credibility of an evaluation's findings and conclusions depend in large part on the credibility of the chosen criteria. Therefore, GAO management pays special attention to the selection of criteria to ensure that they (a) provide clear, objective, and reasonable standards; and (b) are directly relevant, appropriate, and sufficient to answer the evaluation question.

Different evaluation questions imply different values and may draw on different sources of criteria. Some evaluative criteria are specific to a policy area, whereas others apply generally across the federal government. For example, public programs and managers are expected to be transparent and accountable for how they use public resources, to protect public resources from unauthorized use, and to make decisions based on sound evidence. Primary sources of GAO evaluation criteria include:

- Laws and regulations
- U.S. government policy
- Agency standards
- Contract or grant terms
- Best, or good, practices defined through research
- Professional standards and principles
- Social science or economic principles
- Benchmarked performance standards
- Expert opinion
- Previous program performance levels

Federal laws and policies. Assessment criteria for management reviews are often derived from statutes that set government-wide requirements and standards for agency internal accounting, financial management, and administrative control systems. For example, standards GAO issued under the Federal Managers' Financial Integrity Act of 1982 provide a framework for establishing and maintaining internal control over agency management processes, and for identifying and addressing major management challenges and areas of greatest risk of fraud, waste, abuse, and mismanagement (U.S. GAO, 1999).

Compliance assessments involve a clear legal standard as to what activities are or are not authorized and thus have different legal consequences from other types of implementation evaluations. A program's authorizing statute typically defines what activities are required or permitted and often what outcomes are desired. Agencies write regulations to articulate how they will specifically implement provisions of the statute, and these also can serve as evaluative criteria.

The federal government issues a variety of formal policy documents that provide requirements and authoritative guidance for government agencies, and these also can serve as criteria for assessing agency operations. Presidential Directives and Executive Orders describe how agencies are expected to carry out various responsibilities, such as developing a common identification credential across the federal government. OMB, with the federal statistical agencies, has issued standards and guidelines for conducting statistical surveys that can be used to assess the quality of procedures as well as the resulting data (U.S. OMB, 2006).

Professional standards. Other sources of established criteria may provide standards or expectations rather than requirements for program performance. Standards issued by professional organizations, such as the Institute for Electrical and Electronics Engineers, provide numerous standards for specialized technical activities that can serve as evaluative criteria. For example, GAO has used the principles for effective evaluation planning and practice outlined by the American Evaluation Association (AEA) to assess USAID's monitoring and evaluation of foreign assistance (AEA, 2010; U.S. GAO, 2009). GAO evaluators routinely rely on established social science and economic principles in reviewing the quality and credibility of research conducted by agencies and others in order to summarize the available research on a topic or evaluate an agency's own evaluation program.

Benchmarking and expert review. In the absence of acceptable, previously established assessment criteria that analysts can apply to provide a credible, objective answer to the request, GAO may need to develop its own criteria based on measures used in the subject-matter literature, or examples set by other agencies facing the same task. Analyses of practices and characteristics of similar high-performing organizations can provide benchmarks against which to assess performance. Such criteria are typically reviewed by a broad range of subject-area experts for appropriateness and balance. For example, GAO has identified best practices in areas such as business process reengineering through our own observations and analysis of previous research (U.S. GAO, 1997).

Where the evaluative criteria require subjective judgments based on special expertise, GAO may organize a panel of relevant subject-area experts to assess the evidence. To obtain a balanced assessment, a group of experts is selected to represent a wide range of stakeholders and perspectives on the subject, for example, policy analysts, representatives of the affected industry or program participants, and implementing program partners. In some cases, GAO contracts with the National Academies of Sciences to identify and convene such expert panels.

Selecting Credible and Appropriate Criteria

Many congressional requests clearly specify the assessment criteria to be used; they may ask whether program activities and expenditures are in compliance with authorizing law or regulation, or whether improvements in specific outcomes have been achieved. In such cases, the request often provides a sufficiently clear standard or criterion to permit objective assessment. However, in cases where neither the request nor legislative language provide a clear, measurable standard of desired program performance, GAO analysts will initiate clarifying discussions to identify what specific program features or outcomes the requester has in mind. In the course of planning a study, GAO analysts review the program's authorizing legislation and legislative history, previous studies, and policy discussions to understand the policy context and identify available data sources, criteria, and measures that have been used before. Broad questions such as "How effective is the program?" are typically revised to "To what extent is the program achieving its objectives to improve conditions A or B?"

GAO analysts discuss the choice of evaluative criteria with both the congressional requester and agency officials in order to ensure they consider the selected criteria appropriate for answering the request question. If a program has multiple goals, such as increasing both access to and quality of health care, GAO and the requester may decide to broaden the study question to identify what is known about the program's effectiveness on the full set of goals, if practical, or acknowledge the decision to limit the study's scope. If acceptable criteria cannot be found for conducting an objective assessment in response to the original request, GAO and the requester will negotiate a research question for which objective criteria can be identified. However, if no appropriate, objective evaluative criteria can be found, GAO and the requester may agree to replace an evaluative question with a description of conditions or actions taken by the agency.

Problems in Assessing Overall Program Value or Worth

Recently, in efforts to reduce the size of the federal government, policy makers have called for comprehensive rigorous program evaluations to ascertain program effectiveness or overall value, so that they can focus federal funds on programs that work and fix or end those that don't work. However, it is extremely difficult for nonpartisan, nonideological evaluators committed to conducting objective, fact-based assessments to reach an overall conclusion about a program's value. GAO does not make summative evaluative judgments of a program or agency's value or merit for two basic reasons: (a) a summative assessment requires a political decision to prioritize some components of performance (and criteria) over others, and (b) most program assessments are designed for a particular policy purpose, and thus the choice of criteria applies to the specific situation, not overall.

Prioritizing Components of Performance

As described above, there are a variety of dimensions on which to assess program performance: competence of agency management, compliance with statutes and conformance to design expectations, and effectiveness in achieving intended outcomes. Prioritizing these performance elements to create a summative assessment requires policy choices—even how to weigh compliance with program-specific statutes versus compliance with government-wide statutes. These choices can be driven by program features and circumstances and stakeholder interests. In some programs, success may be commonly defined as efficient payment of the correct benefit amounts to eligible participants. In other programs, some inefficiency may be tolerated in return for achieving greater impacts for beneficiaries.

Assessing the effectiveness of a federal program often requires a policy choice among multiple definitions of a program's objectives. In some cases, to accommodate diverse stakeholders' interests, legislation is drafted espousing either (a) very general goals that each stakeholder can interpret according to their own interests, or (b) multiple, sometimes conflicting, goals. For example, the National Park Service is tasked with multiple goals: the preservation and management of the country's natural, historical, and recreational resources. The Service must try to balance not only the competing interests of human visitors and wildlife, but also the competing interests of human visitors with different recreational interests, such as the use of snowmobiles in wilderness areas. Even where goals may not be in conflict, a summative program assessment would require a choice of how to weigh the results on these goals, and stakeholders may disagree on that choice.

The weighting or prioritization of criteria or values is in essence a political decision, assigning priority to some values over others. GAO, as an audit agency, is charged with providing objective, nonpartisan, nonideological analyses, which precludes it from making these political choices. Instead, GAO will report its conclusions on each criterion separately, allowing the diverse stakeholder audiences to weigh the results and develop their own summative conclusions.

Evaluation's Purpose Drives Choice of Criteria

Another challenge to forming an overall summative conclusion about a program's value is that the choice of evaluative criteria depends on the context of a particular decision. Evaluation questions differ, of course, reflecting the nature of the management or policy decisions they are intended to influence: program management or accountability, or policy or budgetary choices. Program managers responsible for day-to-day management often look for evaluations with an internal, process focus to monitor the activities and outputs of agency personnel, grantees, and contractors. Their evaluations, and those designed to serve routine oversight, may make comparisons to rules and standards, agency performance goals, or past performance. Managers may also compare the operations and effectiveness of different program actors or approaches to learn how to improve performance.

For policy discussions of the most effective approach for addressing a policy issue, a useful summative program assessment would not simply compare a program to its own standards and objectives, but would compare it to the performance—management, implementation, and results—of an alternative approach. The alternative might be another type of service (job training vs. subsidized work experience), or another type of policy tool (tax incentives vs. grants for public housing). However, systematic head-to-head comparisons of program alternatives are challenged by lack of comparable data on several dimensions of performance. For example: Does one program appear more effective than the second, but serve only a subset of the intended population? GAO's recent report identifying potential areas of duplication and overlap in federal programs found few areas where there was sufficient information to identify the extent of actual duplication among them (U.S. GAO, 2011). There is a significant potential for bias in drawing conclusions about comparative advantage in the absence of parallel information on performance.

In federal budget discussions—especially when planning spending reductions—a program is likely to be compared to spending on another problem altogether. OMB and the Congress are directly engaged in making budgetary allocation decisions between programs and agencies that involve comparing the "value" of one program to another. In this type of comparison, a summative judgment of a program's overall value includes not only assessing program performance but also the value of the program's stated purpose—that is, the importance of the problem it addresses relative to another problem or program area—for example, housing affordability versus food safety. Setting priorities—considering whether one program serves a more or less important need or constituency than another program—is an inherently subjective, political decision. In a representative democracy, such decisions are the province of an elected or presidential-appointed official, not the auditor or evaluator.

Efforts to Assess Overall Program Value or Worth

GAO's Comprehensive Evaluation Framework

To address the problem of inconsistencies in the evaluative criteria used in many comparisons of policy and program alternatives, several years ago GAO developed a framework of 10 evaluative criteria that Congress could use to compare the value of diverse federal programs serving children and families (U.S. GAO, 1988). The criteria were developed from a review of the program evaluation literature and validated through review by a number of evaluation methodology experts. The 10 general criteria are organized under a framework of three fundamental values in assessing public programs and policies—program need, implementation, and effects:

- Need for the program
  - Problem magnitude
  - Problem seriousness
  - Duplication
- Implementation of the program
  - Interrelationships
  - Program fidelity
  - Administrative efficiency

- Effects of the program
  - Targeting success
  - Achievement of intended objectives
  - Cost effectiveness
  - Other effects

The framework was intended to be used by both technical and policy-making staff together to ensure a comprehensive and balanced program review. Policy-making expertise is required at first to reach agreement on the purpose and scope of the review, prioritize the general criteria, and select relevant indicators for each to match the purpose of the review. Both methodological and substantive expertise is required to ensure that the information collected for a review is credible and applies to the current situation. Technical expertise is required to assess and synthesize available information on the criteria, but substantive expertise is required to combine judgments on several criteria to form an overall assessment of the program. As we noted then, forming an overall assessment of the merit of a program across these criteria is an inherently judgmental process that should be guided by the initial prioritization of the criteria by policy makers.

OMB's Program Assessment Rating Tool (PART)

From 2003–2007, OMB conducted comprehensive assessments of about 1,000 programs across the federal government with the use of its own Program Assessment Rating Tool (PART). The PART represented an effort to standardize the kinds of informal assessments that OMB budget examiners conduct in the process of developing the President's annual budget proposal. The PART consists of 25 standard questions concerning program purpose and design, strategic planning and goal setting, program management (including efficiency), and program results, to be answered by drawing on agency performance data and available evaluations. Based on a weighted average of scores, each program was then characterized as effective, moderately effective, adequate, or ineffective; a fifth rating, results not demonstrated, indicated that OMB found the program's performance information or measures inadequate (U.S. GAO, 2005).

The PART ratings and rating process were highly controversial and demonstrate the inherent challenges in assigning an overall rating of a program's effectiveness. In fact, disagreement over how OMB examiners derived the PART scores primarily accounts for why PART ratings were generally not accepted or used by agencies or, most especially, the Congress (U.S. GAO, 2005). Critics disagreed with the criteria used for judging the programs—both the appropriateness of questions and the choice of outcome measures—and faulted a uniform process for failing to accommodate the wide variation in size and scope among federal programs. Agency officials also questioned

NEW DIRECTIONS FOR EVALUATION • DOI: 10.1002/ev

the competence and technical expertise of OMB budget examiners to assess the quality and relevance of performance and evaluation information. But perhaps most important, many congressional stakeholders distrusted the rating process as politically motivated and objected to not being consulted on the development of the rating tool or the choice of criteria for evaluating program performance.

Conclusions

To conclude, different types of evaluation questions imply different types of criteria for assessing program performance, which could include agency management, program implementation, or effectiveness. Stakeholders may apply different criteria because they have different interests and decisions to make, which lead them to ask different questions about program performance. Judgments of overall program value or merit inevitably involve political decisions to prioritize some aspects of performance over others or judge the program's importance relative to other policy alternatives. It is the evaluator's responsibility to explore and understand these issues with the evaluation's clients and stakeholders, as well as to affirm that the criteria chosen will be credible to the expected evaluation users—those making and carrying out program policy or management decisions, or those affected by those decisions.

References

American Evaluation Association. (2010). *An evaluation roadmap for a more effective government.* Fairhaven, MA.

U.S. Government Accountability Office. (1988). *Children's programs: A comparative evaluation framework and five illustrations.* Washington, DC.

U.S. Government Accountability Office. (1997). *Business process reengineering assessment guide—Version 3.* Washington, DC.

U.S. Government Accountability Office. (1999). *Standards for internal control in the federal government.* Washington, DC.

U.S. Government Accountability Office. (2005). *Performance budgeting: PART focuses attention on program performance but more can be done to engage Congress.* Washington, DC.

U.S. Government Accountability Office. (2009). *International food assistance: USAID is taking actions to improve monitoring and evaluation of nonemergency food aid, but weaknesses in planning could impede efforts.* Washington, DC.

U.S. Government Accountability Office. (2011). *Opportunities to reduce potential duplication in government programs, save tax dollars, and enhance revenue.* Washington, DC.

U.S. Office of Management and Budget. (2006). *Standards and guidelines for statistical surveys.* Washington, DC.

STEPHANIE SHIPMAN *is assistant director of the Center for Evaluation Methods and Issues at the U.S. Government Accountability Office and a member of the American Evaluation Association's Evaluation Policy Task Force.*

6

When One Must Go: The Canadian Experience With Strategic Review and Judging Program Value

François Dumaine

Abstract

This chapter reviews the Canadian experiment with assessing the worth of public programs and policies and using the resulting value judgments to drive funding decisions. The author provides a brief overview of the Canadian Strategic Review initiative, and considers implications of this federal government approach to valuation. The author argues that never before has the evaluation function within the federal government been so directly linked to an expenditure management system that requires such a definitive valuation of programs and initiatives. The author concludes that for the evaluation function to meet expectations and maintain its fundamental purpose of being a participatory process to assist program managers in learning and improving their programs, some fine-tuning will be necessary. © Wiley Periodicals, Inc., and the American Evaluation Association.

The inclusion of the Strategic Review initiative in the Canadian government's 2007 budget was not exactly history in the making. Attempting to control spending, in some form or another, had long been part of the federal government's popular culture. And yet, something different happened that year. For the first time, the program evaluation function was being formally recruited to determine the worth of individual programs and initiatives. This chapter reviews the Canadian experiment with assessing the worth of public programs and policies and using the resulting value judgments to drive funding decisions. I begin with a brief overview of the Canadian Strategic Review, and then consider implications of this federal government approach to valuation.

Understanding the Strategic Review

Put simply, the strategic review is a mandatory process that requires every federal department to assess, on a 4-year cycle, all its direct program spending, as well as the operating costs of its statutory programs. Direct program spending includes financial contributions that the federal government makes to third-party delivery organizations, allowing them to offer a wide range of programs and services, such as settlement programs for new immigrants, federal support to Canadian athletes, research grants, or health programming for Aboriginal communities living on reserve, to name but a very few. Direct program spending also includes the ongoing operating and capital spending that departments require to function, including those resources required to *deliver* statutory programs, such as unemployment insurance or the Canada Pension Plan. It is important to note that actual statutory transfers to individuals or to other orders of governments are systematically excluded from the strategic review process. This exclusion is significant, as major transfers to other orders of governments and to Canadians represented $126 billion in 2009–2010 out of a total budget of $245 billion in program expenditures for the federal government (Department of Finance Canada, 2011, p. 185).

The set of parameters surrounding strategic reviews include two critical conditions. First, all strategic reviews must address the seven key questions included in Table 6.1. Second—and this is by far the most contentious aspect—all departments undertaking a strategic review "are required to identify reallocation options totaling 5% from their lowest-priority, lowest-performing program spending" (Treasury Board of Canada Secretariat, 2011a). During the first 3 years of implementation (2007–2009), the federal

Table 6.1. Strategic Review Questions

1. Is the program a government priority?
2. Is the program consistent with core federal roles?
3. Does the societal need for which the program was designed still exist?
4. Is the program achieving expected results?
5. Is the program achieving results efficiently?
6. Can improvements be made to internal services to maximize efficiencies?
7. Are there opportunities to reduce overlap and duplication to achieve greater efficiencies and savings?

government's goal consisted in rechanneling this 5% of program resources toward better-performing programs or emerging priority areas, within the same department or in other departments. In 2010, as a result of the economic downturn and the impact it has had on budgetary deficits, the savings from the strategic review have not been reinvested, and have rather contributed to the government's deficit-reduction efforts.

The year 2010 marked the fourth round of strategic reviews and, in accordance with the 4-year cycle tempo, all program expenditures covered by the strategic reviews have now been assessed once. The federal government estimates that, in addition to the reallocations that occurred, this first full cycle provided more than $2.8 billion in ongoing savings (Department of Finance Canada, 2011, p. 13). In 2011, the federal government unveiled an additional one-time Strategic and Operating Review that is expected to find $4 billion of permanent annual savings by 2014–2015 (Treasury Board Secretariat, 2011b).

There is not a predefined process or methodology that federal departments must follow when undertaking their strategic review. It is up to each department to determine how they intend to address the seven questions and identify the 5% of lowest-priority, lowest-performing programs to be cut in favor of reallocations or direct savings. In this context, federal departments have had to learn by doing, creating their own templates and establishing a web of internal procedures and committees that have fed information to the highest levels of management within the organization and have had to build their case to be presented to central agencies for consideration and, ultimately, for approval.

As departments designed their own approach to conducting strategic reviews, program evaluation data quickly emerged as an important, yet not unique, source of information. Audit reports, management accountability framework assessments, and reports from the Auditor General of Canada are among the several other sources of information that have been considered to tackle the set of strategic review requirements. For example, the federal government introduced the Management Accountability Framework in 2004 to better frame and assess management strength within each department. The framework focuses on 10 core management disciplines, along with 21 indicators, which are used for yearly assessments.

The Evolving Role of Program Evaluation

As program evaluation data are being used to feed strategic reviews, it is worth exploring the extent to which the program evaluation function is actually suited for this role.

Over the past five decades, every political party that formed the federal government in Canada has attempted to establish its own process to review and control government expenditures. For the longest time, the question of determining how program evaluation data could be used for this purpose was simply irrelevant, as the evaluation function at the federal level had been largely stuck in a slow hatching phase, riding decisively under the radar. Canada's central agency responsible for the operation of government, the Treasury Board of Canada Secretariat, eventually published a circular in 1977 and a *Guide on Program Evaluation* in 1981, urging departments and agencies to undertake a "systematic gathering of verifiable information on programs and demonstrable evidence on their results and cost-effectiveness" (Treasury Board of Canada Secretariat, 1981), but efforts to this end remained largely tentative.

In fact, the program evaluation model that emerged in the late 1970s and that evolved through the 1980s and 1990s appeared ill suited for contributing, to any significant degree, to government-wide program reviews. Evaluations had essentially been operating at the microlevel, focused on improving individual programs. As a result, not all programs within a specific department were evaluated. Instead, federal departments typically identified programs that could benefit from an evaluation and focused their limited resources dedicated for evaluation toward those initiatives. This made it impossible to aggregate all evaluation reports and get a complete picture of a specific department's performance.

In the current context of strategic reviews, the reality is dramatically different. Requirements for program evaluations within the federal government are both systematic and broad. Since 2006 (the same year that the strategic review was launched), there is, for the first time, a legislative obligation on the part of all federal departments to evaluate all their grants and contributions on a 5-year cycle. Section 42.1 of the *Financial Administration Act* now stipulates that "every department shall conduct a review every five years of the relevance and effectiveness of each ongoing program for which it is responsible." In the context of this act, "program" only includes grants and contributions. For some federal departments, this new legislated obligation has meant serious business, as they carry large volumes of grants and contributions programs.

Moreover, since April 2009, the federal government has been implementing a new *Policy on Evaluation* that modifies several aspects of the evaluation function. First, the federal government has established its own working definition of program evaluation that is largely focused on *value for money*: "In the Government of Canada, evaluation is the systematic collection and analysis of evidence on the outcomes of programs to make judgments about their relevance, performance and alternative ways to deliver them or to achieve the same results" (Treasury Board of Canada Secretariat, 2009). More specifically, "evaluation provides Canadians, Parliamentarians, Ministers, central agencies and deputy heads an evidence-based, neutral assessment of the value for money, i.e. relevance and performance, of federal government programs" (Treasury Board of Canada Secretariat, 2009).

Second, the federal government has formally linked program evaluation to strategic reviews. To this end, evaluation "informs government decisions on resource allocation and reallocation by supporting strategic reviews of existing program spending" (Treasury Board of Canada Secretariat, 2009). This is a significant development, as the evaluation function is expected to be structured in such a way as to be in a position to address the seven questions included in Table 6.1.

Third, as a result of being formally linked to the strategic review process, the reach of the evaluation policy now reflects precisely that of the Strategic Review initiative. Hence, all direct program spending and the administrative aspect of major statutory spending must be evaluated every 5 years. This comes on top of the legislative requirement previously mentioned that all programs of grants and contribution be evaluated every 5 years. In light of this, the question is no longer about what needs to be evaluated among a department's set of activities, but rather what activities do not need to be assessed, if any. The Department of Justice Canada offers a good illustration of this new reality. Over time, the department has implemented a number of grants and contributions programs, including some financial support for legal aid services, victims of crimes assistance services, Aboriginal justice initiatives, etc. These have been regularly evaluated. But one of the most fundamental activities undertaken by the Department of Justice Canada, namely, the provision of legal advice to all other federal departments, had never been evaluated. Under the new policy, such activities must now be evaluated on a 5-year cycle. This is but one example of this new evaluation reality that has emerged within the federal government. Evaluating the ongoing provision of legal advice triggers a whole new set of methodological challenges. For instance, establishing the program logic behind such activities, particularly the expected outcomes, forces one to enter unchartered waters, as the actual impact of legal advice on the achievement of federal goals and objectives is determined, to a great extent, by a complex set of factors that are mainly beyond the control of the Department of Justice. Moreover, collecting data in a world dominated by the solicitor–client privilege forces the evaluator to be remarkably creative.

Finally, the *Directive on the Evaluation Function*, which the federal government has adopted to complement the *Policy on Evaluation*, defines a minimum set of issues that each federal evaluation is expected to address, which are presented in Table 6.2.

Tackling New Evaluation Requirements

To meet this expanded coverage of evaluation requirements, and to provide evidence in support of strategic reviews, federal departments had to rethink their internal planning of evaluation activities. The status quo, meaning evaluations of each individual program, could hardly be considered sustainable, for two main reasons. First, there are too many programs and initiatives to be evaluated, and aggregating findings from individual evaluation

Table 6.2. Issues to Be Addressed in Federal Evaluations

Relevance

Issue 1: Continued need for program	Assessment of the extent to which the program continues to address a demonstrable need and is responsive to the needs of Canadians
Issue 2: Alignment with government priorities	Assessment of the linkages between program objectives and (a) federal government priorities and (b) departmental strategic outcomes
Issue 3: Alignment with federal roles and responsibilities	Assessment of the role and responsibilities for the federal government in delivering the program

Performance (Effectiveness, Efficiency, and Economy)

Issue 4: Achievement of expected outcomes	Assessment of progress toward expected outcomes (including immediate, intermediate, and ultimate outcomes) with reference to performance targets and program reach, program design, including the linkage and contribution of outputs to outcomes
Issue 5: Demonstration of efficiency and economy	Assessment of resource utilization in relation to the production of outputs and progress toward expected outcomes

Source: Treasury Board of Canada Secretary, Directive on the Evaluation Function.

reports would be unworkable. Second, departments do not have the level of resources needed for such an endeavor.

In response, many federal departments have undertaken a reorganization of their evaluation plans, and to this end, have initiated higher-level evaluations that assess a grouping of programs and activities, as opposed to microevaluations that focus on a single program. And to guide this grouping process, departments have used a bureaucratic tool known as the program activity architecture (PAA). In essence, the PAA is part of a broader management, resources, and results structure that each department is expected to prepare. Its main purpose is to demonstrate how a series of programs and activities, taken as a whole, align with specific departmental strategic outcomes. This alignment is expected to support and facilitate a number of management requirements, including performance measurement and evaluation. For instance, a department may have a series of programs and activities that aim to support efforts by Canadian businesses and families to make more sustainable use of nonrenewable sources of energy. A traditional approach would consist in evaluating these programs separately. Having a PAA provides an opportunity to engage in an evaluation process whereby all these programs and activities are considered as a cluster. However, such an approach must reconcile the need to assess at a higher level, while providing information that is specific enough to facilitate discussions related to a strategic review.

NEW DIRECTIONS FOR EVALUATION • DOI: 10.1002/ev

Methodological Ramifications

Evidently, expectations under both the evaluation policy and the Strategic Review initiative have had methodological ramifications. For one thing, it has further entrenched the long-standing tradition in Canada of avoiding evaluation studies that focus on measuring net program impacts through experimental design. As an illustration, despite geographical and institutional proximity between evaluators in the United States and Canada, the issue of whether randomized controlled trials should constitute the gold standard when it comes to assessing program impacts has never triggered debates in Canada that even come close to what is seen in the United States. Not only do evaluation time frames and budgets rarely allow for such studies in Canada to occur, but even if they were to be undertaken, it is doubtful that they would actually provide the type of data needed for strategic review purposes. To some extent, this approach is similar to the one applied by the U.S. Government Accountability Office (GAO), as described by Stephanie Shipman in this issue. As an external agent to program delivery and operations, the GAO is typically not in a position to use experimental design to measure program efficiency.

I would argue that what decision makers in Canada predominantly wish to establish is whether a certain cluster of programs is still reflecting a government priority and, if so, whether it rests on the most efficient program structure. Decision makers also wish to know about program results, but expectations are largely focused on determining whether program activities can reasonably be expected to contribute to the expected results, rather than measuring the net impact of these programs. Issue 4 under the directive on the evaluation function calls for an "assessment of *progress* toward expected outcomes (. . .) with reference to performance targets and program reach, program design, including the linkage and *contribution* of outputs to outcomes" (emphasis added). The notions of *progress* and *contribution to outcomes* are used in their broader sense. Indeed, the expectation is not that evaluators will actually measure the extent of the linkage and the net contribution of a program to a set of predefined outcomes. Instead, evaluation studies tend to explore whether a reasonable logic can be established that would link program activities and outputs to a set of predefined outcomes, thus confirming that should the program be implemented effectively, it can reasonably be expected to make a contribution toward those outcomes.

For many evaluators and social sciences purists, this seems a rather watered-down approach, settling for too little when more impact measurement could be done. But this raises the more fundamental question of evaluation use. For senior managers within the federal government, putting all the resources needed (including a reasonable time frame) to measure the net impact of a program is simply not meeting their information needs. As a next cycle of strategic reviews raises its not-so-pretty head, these senior managers need to position themselves by getting a strong sense of which

NEW DIRECTIONS FOR EVALUATION • DOI: 10.1002/ev

programs are resting on solid ground (by reflecting a government priority and performing reasonably well) and which ones are losing traction.

With these considerations in mind, evaluators must construct their knowledge with the use of different reference points. Their selected methods must allow for a clear reading of the current organizational culture within a department, the performance level of processes in place to produce outputs, and the extent to which the program logic rests on sound premises and principles. To achieve this, evaluators must have a broad access to key decision makers, and to performance data and process information that will allow them to make an assessment of the overall strength of a cluster of programs. Needless to say, this is a challenge that evaluators involved in federal evaluations are still struggling with.

New Stakes

I would argue that the launching of the Strategic Review initiative, along with a transformed expenditure management system and a new *Policy on Evaluation*, will profoundly alter the purpose of program evaluation at the federal government level. And with this shift in purposes also comes a new alignment of stakeholders.

It would be foolish to believe that program evaluation at the federal level has always had a clear purpose. Technically speaking, program evaluation has consistently been presented as a management tool, made available to program staff and senior bureaucrats in order to help them improve the effectiveness and impact of their respective programs and initiatives. The actual story has not unfolded as neatly. Program evaluations have typically been undertaken at a time when a program has entered its renewal phase. In fact, evaluation reports have regularly been included in appendices to submissions to the Cabinet made in the interest of funding renewal. In the best-case scenario, departmental managers could agree to have the strengths and weaknesses of their programs documented, and to use the renewal phase to demonstrate how any of the documented shortfalls could be addressed. In other scenarios, departmental managers have systematically shut down any notion of a meaningful introspection on its programming, being instead focused entirely on building a strong case for program renewal. In many ways, the overall departmental culture has to determine the extent to which evaluations could play the intended role of feeding the policy process with evidence-based information.

Now that the first cycle of strategic reviews has been completed, some lessons are emerging. First, a case could be made that perceptions toward the program evaluation function are quickly being transformed, and not necessarily for the better. As evaluation reports are steadily used to feed strategic reviews, there is little doubt on the potential impact of an evaluation report calling for significant improvements to what may be a worthwhile program. This could turn out to be the strongest signal that such a program is dangerously moving into the 5% elimination zone. At the end of the day, something ought to go, and evaluation reports are expected to help chase down lower-performing programs. In this context, is evaluation becoming simply a test that program managers either pass or fail? Is anything but a stellar evaluation report becoming a genuine threat to the very existence of a program? If this was to become a widely shared view, it could turn meaningful evaluation processes into an almost impossible mission. Summarizing the worth of a program on the basis of a single score is something that has been tried in the United States, through the Program Assessment Rating Tool (PART), and as Stephanie Shipman explains in this issue, this approach has proven highly controversial, and has largely been discredited.

Valuing Programs at the Federal Level—Some Observations

As the program evaluation function continues its tentative journey alongside the Canadian Strategic Review initiative, the experience gained to date offers worthwhile insights into the valuing process of federal programs and initiatives. Keeping in mind that there is now a strict alignment between the seven strategic review questions (see Table 6.1) and the core evaluation issues to be addressed at the federal level (see Table 6.2), we can further explore some of the broader impacts that strategic reviews are having on valuing federal programs.

The first and third strategic review questions explore the extent to which a specific program reflects a government priority and addresses a societal need. As one can expect, these two questions do not always align themselves nicely. A program may respond to a well-documented need while not being part of the priorities of the government of the day. More dicey is the scenario where a program may no longer address a clearly defined need and yet falls within the list of government's priorities. Determining the extent to which a program addresses a societal need requires an in-depth analysis, typically conducted through a formal literature review. Assessing the extent to which a program falls within the government's priorities is a simpler proposition, and requires a straightforward review of government's official documentation, along with perhaps a limited number of interviews with government officials. In an environment of limited resources and contracted time frames, one could argue that few evaluations meaningfully address the issue of social needs, and largely confine themselves to a matching of program goals with government priorities.

The second strategic review question in Table 6.1 brings up the typical Canadian question of roles and responsibilities between the federal and provincial governments. Our modern society, with its complex web of programs and initiatives, has pretty much evacuated the notion of a clear distinction between the roles and responsibilities of our two orders of government. More often than not, evaluators are dragged into muddy waters, whereby a strong rationale in favor of a strong federal intervention may exist, or inversely, that provinces have exclusive jurisdictions and should therefore be allowed to operate independently. Yet again, this is an issue where finding a clear-cut answer is the exception rather than the rule.

Then comes the issue of effectiveness, and the notion of economy (see issue 5 in Table 6.2). In many ways, this is where valuing programs is considered at its most fundamental expression. Serious limitations in relation to both resources and time frame have already made it challenging to assess the effectiveness of a program (the extent to which it achieves its expected results). Summative evaluation processes at the federal level rarely extend beyond 8–10 months, which limits the ability to implement a genuinely mixed-method approach. Digging into the issue of effectiveness (the extent to which results are achieved with the lowest level of resources) is an even more daunting task. As stated in issue 5 (in Table 6.2), evaluations are expected to assess the "resource utilization in relation to the production of outputs and progress toward expected outcomes." The Treasury Board of Canada Secretariat is currently developing a guide to assist evaluators in tackling the *economy* issue. Perhaps there is a theoretically sound approach to assessing resource utilization to produce the required outputs leading up to the expected results, but such analyses raise formidable logistical challenges. The evaluator's capacity to access detailed financial and operational data to assess resource utilization at a micro level will require a fundamental shift in the current organizational culture of the federal government.

One could argue that never before has the evaluation function within the federal government been so directly linked to an expenditure management system that requires such a definitive valuation of programs and initiatives. When one must go, as the feared 5% rule requires, there cannot only be winners. To respond to this challenge, evaluation is forced to assess an ever-larger cluster of programs and initiatives, and to this day appears to be struggling to produce the data required for senior bureaucrats making these difficult decisions. As this undertaking continues to unfold, the stakes are high for the function itself. For the evaluation function to meet expectations of this nature and magnitude, while maintaining its fundamental purpose of being a participatory process to assist program managers in learning and improving their programs, some fine threading will be required.

References

Department of Finance Canada. (2011). *The next phase of Canada's Economic Action Plan: A low-tax plan for jobs and growth.* Ottawa, Canada.

Treasury Board of Canada Secretariat. (1981). *Guide on the program evaluation function.* Ottawa, Canada.

Treasury Board of Canada Secretariat. (2009). *Policy on evaluation.* Retrieved from http://www.tbs-sct.gc.ca/pol/doc-eng.aspx?section=text&id=15024

Treasury Board of Canada Secretariat. (2011a). *Strategic reviews*. Retrieved from http://www.tbs-sct.gc.ca/sr-es/faq-eng.asp

Treasury Board of Canada Secretariat. (2011b). *Address by Minister Tony Clement to public service executives at APEX Symposium*. Retrieved from http://www.tbs-sct.gc.ca /media/ps-dp/2011/0608-eng.asp

FRANÇOIS DUMAINE *is a partner at PRA (Prairie Research Associates) Inc., a firm specializing in program evaluation, and the past president of the Canadian Evaluation Society.*

Chelimsky, E. (2012). Valuing, evaluation methods, and the politicization of the evaluation process. In G. Julnes (Ed.), *Promoting valuation in the public interest: Informing policies for judging value in evaluation*. New Directions for Evaluation, 133, 77–83.

7

Valuing, Evaluation Methods, and the Politicization of the Evaluation Process

Eleanor Chelimsky

Abstract

The author argues that valuing is often about methodology, or questions about how to measure the value of a public program or policy, including how we measure the factual underpinnings of programs and how we synthesize information about issues relevant to public programs and policies. The organizational context is discussed as an important determinant of what methods are used, and that these decisions have become increasingly influenced by a single narrative—a narrative that sees increasing numbers of government programs and policies embodying a single idea, or positing a simple, one-on-one cause-and-effect relationship, both of which are established, not by evidence, but rather by suppressing existing evidence that is inconvenient to the particular idea or relationship being advanced. The implications of this single narrative on methodology are discussed and ways forward described. © Wiley Periodicals, Inc., and the American Evaluation Association.

As Raymond Carver might ask, what do we talk about when we talk about valuing? To me, it seems that valuing, like Carver's version of loving, is complex, diffuse, emotionally laden, and loaded with euphemisms, but that it boils down in the end to some pretty prosaic questions (Carver, 1988). For evaluators, one question might be, how do we measure the value of a public program or policy? Or else, how do we measure its factual underpinnings, the truth of assertions made to rationalize it?

Or even, how do we synthesize all the knowledge available on a given issue? In short, what we are talking about when we talk about valuing is methodology, and we evaluators have spent a lot of time and effort trying to get it right.

Stronger methods allow us more confidence in the value judgments we make about a particular intervention, and weaker ones (which may be the only alternatives feasible in a particular design situation) force us to pepper those judgments with needed caveats. Our big problem is that we cannot always choose the strongest methodology per se. The type of evaluation question posed—seeking to assess, say, (a) the merit or worth of some initiative (which would make it an accountability question), or (b) the state of existing research underlying an initiative and its subject matter (which would make it a knowledge question), or (c) the current or changing size of some population or public problem (which would make it a descriptive question)—will largely determine which methods are appropriate for a particular evaluation, based also, however, on the historical, political, and evaluative context of the subject matter. This means, of course, not only that choosing methods for valuing is a complicated process, but also that those methods may be used for fact finding, or truth telling, as well as for establishing merit or worth.

Agency Involvement With Particular Methods

Some evaluative methods have benefited from various periods of vogue in different government agencies. For example, cost/benefit analysis was an important component of the Department of Defense's Planning, Programming and Budgeting System in the sixties; randomized controlled designs were favored by the Office of Economic Opportunity and other agencies for social program demonstrations in the sixties and seventies (as well as more recently, by the Department of Education); and the case-study method was the rock on which the Government Accountability Office built its evaluations over a period of decades.

Unfortunately, these methods, like all evaluation methods, suffer from warts and flaws that make them inappropriate for some evaluation questions (Chelimsky, 2007). For example, the randomized controlled design, which can be very strong for establishing the effectiveness of an intervention in one place (internal validity), does not normally bring evidence, without the use of additional methods, as to whether that intervention will be effective somewhere else (external validity). Cost/benefit studies are usually pretty good at predicting either costs or benefits, given an adequate basis in past evaluations, but there have been stubborn problems in getting agreement on definitions of costs and benefits. In addition, these studies have suffered from variability in their results when costs or benefits are hard to quantify, and when costs are short-term and benefits long-term, or vice versa (Chelimsky,

1977). As for the case study, which brings detailed information to illuminate a specific instance, it can be generalized only at some risk to the evaluator. Even with a careful plan to link a set of case studies together, it may be difficult to generalize because of the infinite variety of local circumstances.

Today, in the summer of 2011, it appears that some agencies still lean on treasured methods. This may be due to habit (the seductions of familiarity with one or another methodological tool), or to an unwillingness to take on the uncertainties involved in matching methods more appropriately to questions, or even, as some suggest, to a general decline in our societal ability to entertain complexity. Still, in some agencies at least, there now seems to be a growing understanding of the strengths and weaknesses implicit in the various evaluation methods for answering a given question, and greater willingness to try a mixed-methods approach that uses the strengths of one (or several) methods to shore up the weaknesses of others. Some of these agencies have benefited, perhaps, from the American Evaluation Association (AEA) publication, "Roadmap for a More Effective Government" (American Evaluation Association, 2010). This can be seen in recent communications on evaluation by the Office of Management and Budget; in the State Department's issuance, last May, of a new policy on evaluation; and the National Institutes of Health's current effort to adapt the Roadmap's evaluation approach to translational research. And there are similar endeavors in the planning stages in other agencies and in the Congress. So there does seem to be some progress in moving toward a more fully explicated use of methods for valuing an intervention.

The Advent of the Single Narrative

On the other hand, the interventions themselves appear to be changing in the opposite direction: that is, they are becoming less, rather than more sophisticated, and more, rather than less political. We are seeing increasing numbers of government programs and policies that embody a single idea, or posit a simple, one-on-one cause-and-effect relationship, both of which are established, not by dint of a preponderance of evidence, but rather by suppressing existing evidence that is inconvenient to the particular idea or relationship being advanced. This is the single narrative, which often results in programs or treatments that feature quite profound distortions of fact and of reality. And because we are often called to evaluate these initiatives, their genesis—and especially the suppression of evidence involved in developing their rationales—has important ramifications for all of our methods. This is to say that if the program or policy is based on invalid premises or assumptions, evaluators are likely to be faced either with a "weak-thrust, weak-effect" situation, or one in which, even with the best possible choice of methods, their evaluations will be answering the wrong questions.

It's true that in the past, evaluators have often complained about government interventions, in particular, the fact that policies and programs were not typically initiated "directly and clearly as an output of research" (Abt, 1977). And of course, they were not. Sometimes they were the product of administrative judgment and experience rather than of research or policy analysis of a public problem. Sometimes they emerged in all their splendid vagueness from the hard-won political consensus required to pass a bill in the Congress (the Bureau of Indian Affairs, for example, once had to develop a legislatively mandated program whose goal was to "improve Indian civilization") (Hemmes, 1977). Sometimes the eccentric idea of an administration official achieved agency implementation with little justification in theory or evidence. However, in a democratic society, it is, in fact, elected officials and agency policymakers, not evaluators, who are charged with developing governmental initiatives. Evaluators have dealt with this situation by pointing out intervention inadequacies in their final reports and by maneuvering to change the evaluation questions, evolve specificity and precision out of vagueness, and ground their findings and recommendations in reality. The main point here, however, is that, in the past, the conceptual weaknesses of programs and policies usually—although not always—came from lack of sophistication, not political purpose.

The Single Narrative and Its Implications for Methodology

Today, however, we are seeing a remarkable expansion of the politically inspired single narrative across a variety of subject areas, with interventions deliberately structured to ask only those questions that will lead to the right, or desired answer. This expansion is occurring not only in the public sector but in the federally regulated private sector as well. Also, the single narrative, which used to operate mostly at the pre-evaluation stage of a program or policy (by constricting the body of knowledge already existing about a public problem, by presenting only one set of facts and views, and by developing an intervention that reifies that truncated version of reality), now increasingly features an additional component that takes place during the actual implementation of the evaluation. As Ernest House has reported, "drug companies have found ways of producing the results they want, including manipulation of treatment (dosages), selection of sample, control of data, and calculated publication" (that is, the selective reporting of favorable findings and the suppression of negative results) (House, 2008). Two points are important here. First, the interferences in the evaluation process reported by House could bring improper compromises and conflicts of interest for the evaluator. And second, these cases show the power of the two political components: the single narrative and the introduction of bias into the evaluation treatment can be effectively deployed at the very heart of evaluation's strongest methodology: the randomized, controlled experimental design.

NEW DIRECTIONS FOR EVALUATION • DOI: 10.1002/ev

Current Expansion of Efforts to Direct and Control Evaluations

One can speculate on the reasons for the current expansion. First, we are clearly at the ideological end of the regular democratic political cycle that moves from incrementalism to ideology and back (Chelimsky, 1996), and many single-narrative programs have been hatched during these periods of ideological fervor (e.g., the Reagan Administration's "Just Say No" program, which reduced adolescent drug problems in America to a series of stereo-types) (Chelimsky, 1996). Second, the combined single-narrative and implementation-control effort no longer needs to rely on improvisation, but benefits today from an effective model for manipulating evidence that was largely unknown in the past. This is the process developed by the Department of Defense in the 1980s and 1990s for presenting only one side of a case (in a budget request, say, for funding a new program or technology) and for using classification and selective reporting to suppress any data that might cast doubt on that presentation (U.S. Government Accountability Office/Program Evaluation and Methodology Division, 1988).

Today, the single narrative is alive and well at the Department of Defense (for example, in the continuing saga favoring piloted vehicles over drones, big technology over small, and bombers over nuclear submarines, despite continuing experience and evidence to the contrary) (Beschloss, 2011). However, we also find the single narrative spreading to health care (not only in the shape of drug companies that refuse to release unfavorable data, but also in the formulation of guidelines for clinical trials and conflicts of interest within "the expert committees reviewing clinical trials and selecting what constitutes 'best evidence'") (Groopman, 2009). We see the narrative again in education (with respect both to unfounded assumptions about charter schools, and the notion that bad teachers are the single cause of poor student outcomes) (Ravitch, 2010). We find it in energy (with the Nuclear Regulatory Commission's assurances of system safety that are presented without discussion of the Commission's loosening or weak-ening of the very safety standards through which indications of lessening safety would emerge) (Donn, 2011); in the environment (with the contin-uing insistence, often heard in the Congress, that climate change is a hoax) (Warner, 2011); and in regulation (e.g., the dismantling of the Glass-Steagall Act, based on the assertions of special banking interests and the suppression of evidence about its long-term public benefits) (Nocera, 2011).

In my judgment, these two political components—the single narrative (with its ability to direct and control the evaluation process) and the manip-ulation of treatment procedures (which nullifies strong methodologies and exposes evaluators to potential conflicts of interest)—present major prob-lems for the evaluative enterprise. At a time when ideological warriors can be expected, as in the past, to cut both public programs and the evaluation systems that inform on their results, in order to reduce the size of government

(Chelimsky, 1985), it may be that the best we can do in the face of the hurricane is to wait for a change in political cycle dynamics toward a more prudent, Jeffersonian incrementalism. But there are, perhaps, a few small things we might do now that could help avoid similar distortions of both the evaluation process and government accountability in the future.

Four Suggestions

1. Given the attention that the AEA's "Roadmap" has been receiving both in federal agencies and in the Congress, it may be useful to amend that document to provide measures for dealing with the evaluation and accountability problems that occur when evaluations are either politically skewed at the start, or improperly manipulated during their implementation.
2. Evaluators should be urged to use their final report, as they have done in the past, to cast light on shadowy areas of program or policy construction and rationale. This can be a successful tactic when the suppression of evidence is egregious, or when there is a powerful constituency that is willing to help in the debate.
3. Standing review panels could be appointed in neutral places like universities to examine cases of interference with evaluative independence during the course of a study, in order to assess damage to evaluation quality in the particular study, and to deter further political efforts in this direction.
4. Finally, the AEA might consider opening an inquiry on this double problem under the aegis of its Ethics Committee. The effort could seek to give guidance to both policy makers and evaluators by examining the role evaluators should play in dealing with political manipulations that threaten the evaluative capability to produce new knowledge about government programs, or to measure their merit and worth.

We could, of course, simply wait and hope for things to improve, but single narratives are pernicious because of the falsehoods and the constricted ways of thinking they embody, and because they have far-reaching effects that are not limited to evaluation. As Hannah Arendt once put it, "Freedom of opinion is a farce unless factual information is guaranteed and the facts themselves are not in dispute" (Arendt, 1967). Indeed, the problem with rigging the evaluation process through the single narrative is precisely that: We do not get all the facts, and the facts we are given may not be facts at all. This affects us in at least three ways: in our ability to think clearly about public problems, in our ability to perform meaningful evaluations, and in our ability to use those evaluations to improve accountability and transparency in government.

References

Abt, C. C. (1977). *Perspectives on the costs and benefits of applied social research* (p. 4). Cambridge, MA: Abt Books.

American Evaluation Association. (2010). *An evaluation roadmap for a more effective government.* Retrieved from http://www.eval.org/EPTF/aea10.roadmap.101910.pdf

Arendt, H. (1967, February 24). Reflections on truth and politics. *The New Yorker,* p. 52.

Beschloss, M. (2011, April 24). Missing the target. *New York Times Book Review,* p. 14.

Carver, R. (1988). *Where I'm calling from.* New York, NY: Vintage Books.

Chelimsky, E. (1977). Perspectives on the costs and benefits of applied social research. In C. C. Abt (Ed.), *Perspectives on the costs and benefits of applied social research* (pp. 179–195). Cambridge, MA: Abt Books.

Chelimsky, E. (1985). Budget cuts, data and evaluation. *Society, 22*(3), 65–73.

Chelimsky, E. (1996). *Distinguished public policy lectures.* Evanston, IL: Center for Urban Affairs and Policy Research, Northwestern University.

Chelimsky, E. (2007). Factors influencing the choice of methods in federal evaluation practice. In G. Julnes & D. J. Rog (Eds.), *Informing federal policies on evaluation methodology. New Directions for Evaluation, 113,* 13–34.

Donn, J. (2011, June 20). NRC loosens, ignores safety rules to keep nuclear reactors operating. *Plain Dealer,* p. 2.

Groopman, J. (2009, November 5). Diagnosis: What doctors are missing. *The New York Review of Books,* p. 26.

Hemmes, R. A. (1977). Evaluation at the Bureau of Indian Affairs. In E. Chelimsky (Ed.), *Proceedings of a symposium on the use of evaluation by federal agencies* (Vol. I, pp. 26–28). Bedford, MA: MITRE.

House, E. R. (2008). Blowback: Consequences of evaluation for evaluation. *The American Journal of Evaluation, 29*(4), 416–418.

Nocera, J. (2011, June 18). The banking miracle. *New York Times,* p. 14.

Ravitch, D. (2010, November 11). The myth of charter schools. *The New York Review of Books,* pp. 22–24.

U.S. Government Accountability Office/Program Evaluation and Methodology Division. (1988). *Weapons testing: Quality of DOD operational testing and reporting* (No. 88–32BR). Washington, DC.

Warner, J. (2011, February 27). Fact-free science. *New York Times Magazine,* p. 11.

ELEANOR CHELIMSKY is an independent consultant for evaluation policy, practice, and methodology and was for 14 years the director of program evaluation and methodology at the U.S. Government Accountability Office. She previously evaluated programs and policies at NATO, and then at the MITRE Corporation.

Morris, M. (2012). Valuation and the American Evaluation Association: Helping 100 flowers bloom, or at least be understood? In G. Julnes (Ed.), *Promoting valuation in the public interest: Informing policies for judging value in evaluation*. New Directions for Evaluation, 133, 85–90.

8

Valuation and the American Evaluation Association: Helping 100 Flowers Bloom, or at Least Be Understood?

Michael Morris

Abstract

The author explores the challenges encountered when organizations attempt to facilitate evaluation and improvement through policy statements of professional associations. The American Evaluation Association (AEA) is used as an example. Various AEA statements are described as general and avoiding particular value preferences. The author concludes there is more that professional associations can do if valuation engagement is desirable, and offers modest recommendations that would facilitate that engagement. © Wiley Periodicals, Inc., and the American Evaluation Association.

Improving public-sector valuation is a worthy goal. It assumes, of course, that we can agree on what "improvement" means in this context. And when the objective is to facilitate improvement through policy positions developed by professional associations or educational institutions, the task of enhancing public-sector valuation can become downright intimidating. This chapter uses the American Evaluation Association (AEA) as an example, explores the challenges that are likely to be encountered when organizations tackle this domain, and offers some tentative recommendations for how those challenges might be addressed.

Multiple perspectives on valuation exist (descriptive, prescriptive, ethical/moral, etc.). Not surprisingly, AEA has avoided taking positions that specifically endorse one valuation stance over another, although it has issued public statements urging policymakers *not* to overemphasize certain criteria when evaluating program performance. In its 2003 statement on high-stakes testing, for example, AEA asserts that "the simplistic application of single tests or test batteries to make high stakes decisions about individuals and groups impede rather than improve student learning" (American Evaluation Association, 2003a, p. 1). The statement goes on to say that "state and local governance of education should draw on a wide range of perspectives as to what is best for students, schools, and society" (p. 3), and that "the most serious problem with high stakes testing is its insistence that education be evaluated in a narrow way" (p. 3). Similar sentiments are expressed in AEA's 2006 Educational Accountability public statement, where the Association cautions against "over-reliance on standardized test scores that are not necessarily accurate measures of student learning" and "definitions of success that require test score increases that are higher or faster than historical evidence suggests is possible" (American Evaluation Association, 2006, p. 1).

An expansive rather than narrow view of success criteria is also evident in AEA's 2009 commentary, *Evaluation and Oversight of Health Care Reforms in the House Discussion Draft Bill*. The commentary identifies at least 21 objectives of the proposed reforms that AEA believes warrant more evaluation attention than the draft bill displayed, such as expansion of community health centers and community-based programs, the addressing of health disparities, and prevention of hospital readmissions. Indeed, the statement recommends the development of an "Annual National Report Card" for health care reform, targeting recurring success measures such as "percent of uninsured persons, health care cost indices, status of meeting modernization goals, and possibly key health status indicators" (American Evaluation Association, 2009, p. 5).

All of the preceding recommendations are consistent with a philosophy, articulated in AEA's *An Evaluation Roadmap for a More Effective Government*, that the federal government should "consult closely with Congress and nonfederal stakeholders in defining program and policy objectives and critical operations and definitions of success" (American Evaluation Association, 2010, p. 5). Viewed as a whole, the implicit message of these pronouncements is that multiple perspectives on valuation should be embraced by the public sector. In this fashion, the potentially thorny problem of deciding on the "one best" criterion to employ in a given evaluation context is finessed. Indeed, from this vantage point, the task of searching for the one best criterion is an ill-advised quest. Interestingly, the spirit of this message can also be seen in AEA's controversial 2003 public statement that critically reviewed the U.S. Department of Education's preference for randomized clinical trials over other designs that could shed light on program impact (American Evaluation Association, 2003b).

With this history in mind, is there more that AEA and other professional associations could do to elevate the quality of discourse concerning public-sector valuation? The answer is almost certainly yes. Taking a page from the House and Howe (1999) deliberative democratic approach, AEA could articulate major perspectives on valuation in ways that make them more accessible to key stakeholders in public-sector decision making. This should be done in both general and specific terms. At the former level, the basic tenets of various perspectives would be described and explained. At the latter, the focus would be on the application of those perspectives to specific policy arenas (education, health care, employment, welfare, criminal justice, etc.). Undertaking these activities would move AEA significantly beyond its current level of official engagement with the topic of valuation.

At both levels, the objectives espoused by AEA would need to be perceived as *educational* in nature if the Association wished to be regarded as a bipartisan wielder of expert power. For those who recall the struggles associated with AEA's early forays into the public policy arena, this represents an ambitious agenda. However, with the establishment of AEA's Evaluation Policy Task Force in 2006, it appears that the Association has developed a mechanism for communicating with government policy makers that produces less internal divisiveness than in the past. Even so, the nature of valuation, focusing as it does on *what* should be evaluated, and not just on *how* to evaluate it, can surface visions of the public interest and welfare that evoke intense, strongly held opinions. Consider, for example, the contrasting perspectives that continue to exist on the success of welfare reform in the United States in the mid-1990s (e.g., Collins & Mayer, 2011; Mead, 2011). Against this background, it is not surprising that AEA's Guiding Principle of Responsibilities for General and Public Welfare does not offer specific definitions of such concepts as "public welfare" or "public good" (see Morris, 2009). The phrase "the devil is in the details" has become a cliché for good reason, and serves as a warning to those wishing to articulate the fine-grained implications of value-based mandates. That being said, what advice might we give to AEA if it chooses to venture further down the path of valuation engagement? I offer five modest recommendations.

1. Begin with the valuation challenges that public-sector decision makers see themselves facing. Addressing the self-perceived needs of stakeholders is a sound, empirically based strategy for capturing their attention. What types of input relevant to valuation are they seeking? If stakeholders do not conceptualize the input they need as valuation-related, how can the topic of valuation be introduced in a way that will be viewed as credible and useful? Understandably, policy makers mainly desire help in answering the questions that they have about programs, rather than the questions that "experts" think they *should be* asking.
2. Broaden the conversation. Stakeholders often view valuation through a narrow lens, subscribing to a particular model (e.g., cost–benefit

analysis) or measure (e.g., standardized achievement test scores) that can omit important considerations in judging program or policy performance. The challenge is to motivate decision makers to take seriously alternative valuation approaches. Abstract discussions are unlikely to succeed. Rather, analyses must be tied to the specific contexts within which these stakeholders are actually approaching decisions. How will the perceived quality of these decisions be enhanced if a broader perspective is adopted? Answering this question in a way that is responsive to the myriad constraints that beleaguered public-sector actors encounter (e.g., in time, resources, and political support) is not easy. Balancing comprehensiveness and thoroughness with focus, conciseness, and pragmatic relevance is required.

3. Acknowledge the role of self-interest. Although policy debates are typically framed in terms suggesting that the sole driving forces are competing visions of the common good, the role that political self-interest plays in those discussions can be, and usually is, crucial. Social policies, as well as indicators of policy effectiveness, can garner support not so much for the values they represent as for the political capital they produce for the stakeholders identified with them. Analyses that acknowledge and explore how these dynamics operate within the context of specific valuation perspectives are sorely needed. For example, cost–benefit approaches can be especially popular during economically troubled periods, even though they may neglect meaningful outcomes that are not easily monetized. By the time the consequences of such neglect become evident to the public, significant political capital may already have been gained, and disputes over "who was responsible for what" are often dominated by multiple revisionist histories.

Depicting how valuation approaches can serve stakeholders' vested interests in various ways is a daunting task. To the greatest extent possible these analyses must be viewed as balanced and even-handed, or the ability of the organizations offering them to affect the way decision makers reflect upon their work will be severely impaired.

4. Be data-driven, not speculation-driven. Valuation and strong emotions are first cousins. As has been noted, beliefs about the criteria that should be used to evaluate policies and programs can be closely tied to deeply held ideological positions about what constitutes the good society. In these circumstances, the temptation to go beyond the data in predicting the consequences, both positive and negative, of one set of criteria being adopted instead of another can be powerful. It is crucial to distinguish between what we know about different valuation approaches and their impacts, and what we regard as plausible, but not verified, conclusions concerning those impacts. Professional associations such as AEA must keep this distinction in mind as they interact with public-sector stakeholders concerning valuation. In instances

where the line between knowing and not quite sure is fuzzy, and it often is, erring on the side of not quite sure is probably the better course of (non)action.

5. Provide stakeholders with opportunities to practice and reflect upon valuation. With AEA's Guiding Principles Training Package (American Evaluation Association, n.d.), which is available at the Association's website, users can apply the Guiding Principles for Evaluators to a case study. Developing a training package focused on major valuation approaches would be a more taxing endeavor, given the absence of an official list of such perspectives, but certainly not an impossible task. The package could include one or more case scenarios to which various valuation frameworks could be applied. This training is likely to increase participants' appreciation of the advantages and disadvantages of various approaches and, one hopes, expand the possibilities they consider when engaging in public-sector valuation. It would be helpful if the package included prioritizing exercises related to the scenarios, in which participants grapple with the challenge of not having sufficient resources, or stakeholder support, to do justice to all of the valuation criteria they would like to employ in an evaluation.

Conclusion

Debates about policies and programs in the United States and elsewhere often devolve into rancorous displays of partisan bickering or worse, lowering the confidence of citizens in the ability of public-sector decision makers to constructively address social issues. Applying the lens of multiple valuation perspectives to these debates will not eliminate them, nor should it, but it could have the salutary effect of making the debates more informed, more civil, and—dare we hope?—more rational. This is a goal worth striving for by any professional association that wishes to contribute to public discourse, including AEA.

References

American Evaluation Association. (n.d.). *AEA guiding principles training package.* Retrieved from http://www.eval.org/GPTraining/GPTrainingOverview.asp

American Evaluation Association. (2003a). *Position statement on high-stakes testing in preK-12 education.* Retrieved from http://www.eval.org/hst3.htm

American Evaluation Association. (2003b). *Response to U.S. Department of Education, "Scientifically based evaluation methods."* Retrieved from http://www.eval.org /doestatement.htm

American Evaluation Association. (2006). *Public statement: Educational accountability.* Retrieved from http://www.eval.org/edac.statement.asp

American Evaluation Association. (2009). *Evaluation and oversight of health care reforms in the House discussion draft bill.* Retrieved from http://www.eval.org/EPTF.asp

American Evaluation Association. (2010). *An evaluation roadmap for a more effective government*. Retrieved from http://www.eval.org/EPTF/aea10.roadmap.101910.pdf

Collins, J. L., & Mayer, V. (2011). Reconfiguring the social contract: A summary of *Both Hands Tied. Focus, 28*(1), 1–6.

House, E. R., & Howe, K. R. (1999). *Values in evaluation and social research*. Thousand Oaks, CA: Sage.

Mead, L. M. (2011). Reactions to *Both Hands Tied. Focus, 28*(1), 6–9.

Morris, M. (2009). The fifth guiding principle: Beacon, banality, or Pandora's box? *American Journal of Evaluation, 30*, 220–224.

MICHAEL MORRIS is a professor of psychology at the University of New Haven; his research focuses on ethical issues in program evaluation.

NEW DIRECTIONS FOR EVALUATION • DOI: 10.1002/ev

Grob, G. F. (2012). Evaluators in a world of valuators. In G. Julnes (Ed.), *Promoting valuation in the public interest: Informing policies for judging value in evaluation. New Directions for Evaluation, 133,* 91–96.

9

Evaluators in a World of Valuators

George F. Grob

Abstract

The author argues that in public policy making, evaluators have no monopoly on valuation, and that public policy decisions in the United States are almost never made by a single person, organizational entity, or profession. The argument is that what distinguishes evaluators from other valuators is a desire to evaluate public programs, hoping that they can find out what works and what doesn't, and then persuade policy makers, program managers, and professional advocates, and a broad citizen readership, to make rational and efficacious decisions. It is evaluators' broad command of valuation theories and practical methods, their independence, and their professional demeanor that makes them so valuable. The author concludes that the best way to preserve professional reputation is to be independent, relevant, helpful, and respectful. © Wiley Periodicals, Inc., and the American Evaluation Association.

When it comes to public policy making, evaluators have no monopoly on valuation. Public policy decisions in the United States at every level—national, state, local—are almost never made by a single person, organizational entity, or profession. The elaborate processes by which public policies are made—legislation, regulations, budget, strategic planning, goal setting, reorganization—involve a dizzying array of stakeholders. Those who make or influence policy for a living—public office holders, professional advocates, major media personalities—are painfully aware that public policy is never made until all the stakeholders have been consulted and either fundamentally agree in principle with the proposed policy or finally realize that such agreement is impossible. Many of them actually feel awful when a decision is forced, because they take pride in finding solutions that most everyone can buy into.

All of them—legislators, executives, managers, advisors, professional analysts of all kinds, advocates, policy analysts, social scientists, influential reporters and media personalities, and (of course) professional evaluators—are valuators. It doesn't matter whether evaluators believe that they are the only trained, professional valuators. All the other policy players just go ahead and valuate away. It is the universality of the valuation function that makes it so powerful in our society, not the studied specialization of one profession that uses this action noun in its self-chosen professional moniker.

And it ought to be that way—the more valuators the better, especially those who know what they are doing. And everyone does. Valuation is a natural human skill, seeing how survival depends on it. It comes instinctively in every human body, even very young and inexperienced ones.

Even untrained valuators do a good job of valuing. So sure are we of this that we remand the most fundamental decisions of our society—to determine the guilt or innocence of the accused, whether a convicted criminal will live or die, and who will represent us in local, state, and federal legislative bodies, executive offices, and in some cases who will judge us—to citizens no matter what their professional education. We would never think of remanding these fundamental valuation questions exclusively to professional evaluators.

Of course, natural talents work better with training and discipline. Valuation is like that. And many, many people are so trained. Almost all white-collar professions teach their adherents the right way to valuate. There is a correct way to determine guilt or innocence, find out if drugs are safe and efficacious, diagnose and treat a patient, determine how much tax to pay, prove a mathematical theorem, test a scientific hypothesis, test a marketing slogan, choose the winning debate team in a college debate tournament, present an issue paper to a policy maker, and evaluate a program. These correct valuation methods are taught in college and refined on the job. Stakeholders on all sides of a policy issue learn how to do this very well.

So how are evaluators different? Well, as a group, they are not less biased, more ethical, or more concerned about the well being of others. They may think they are, but most stakeholders would claim similar traits.

Among the things that distinguish the evaluator from other valuators is a desire to evaluate public programs, hoping that they can find out what works and what does not, and then persuade policy makers, program managers, professional advocates, and a broad citizen readership to make rational and efficacious decisions. (Yes, persuade. Evaluators do not just valuate.)

What we evaluators do best and most distinctively is carefully learn about valuation approaches and methods, reasoning, proof, and evidence.

Other professionals who are trained in valuating are taught a particular way to do it. Evaluators take on this discipline of valuating more broadly, studying all kinds of ways to do it. Individual evaluators may gradually favor and practice in a limited aspect of valuation, but that is not because of their training or because they are denied access to a more sweeping panorama of thinking, logic, and appraisal. Their professional journals (including this one) and national conferences are kaleidoscopic in their treatment of the thinking process.

Actually, we evaluators are a bit obsessive about this business of thinking about valuation. We do it all the time, sometimes boring other professionals within hearing distance of our deliberations. We evaluate how we evaluate. We think about how we think. We think about how others think and evaluate. We do not hesitate to tell our colleagues and even other professional thinkers when we think they are not thinking correctly.

So what does this mean for the evaluator interested in public policy? For one thing, it means that rarely will policy makers ask evaluators to come up with the exclusively correct value of a public program. Instead, they will request plausible answers that they will consider. When an evaluation study is completed, policy makers will provide their comments through an intense but generally productive exchange often leading to the adoption of new policies. What is worthwhile, then, is for the evaluator to ask some additional questions, such as the following.

What Can I Contribute to the Valuating That Unfolds in the Policy-Making Process?

Coaching

One of the most useful things evaluators can add to the policy valuation machinery flows from their strong suit—their profound and facile understanding of all shades and flavors of valuation. Delivered tactfully and professionally, this general set of insights is valuable. Most policy makers and advocates are dealing with extraordinarily difficult issues. If the problems were easy, they wouldn't be issues. If solutions to complex social problems were obvious, then the policy makers and advocates would have already adopted them. The policy-making cadres will be truly grateful if an evaluator can show them some practical directions to explore. The reason they cannot solve these difficult problems is because they are stuck in the conventional patterns of valuation. Practical ways of thinking about complex problems is what they are searching for, and ultimately is their only hope to finding productive paths. In some cases, evaluators may have a much longer menu of options of thinking and valuating options than other trained valuators. So don't be shy about sharing such options.

But don't be arrogant about it, either. The evaluator is not the high school sports coach. These are highly trained professionals they are dealing with. Cultivate a professional tone that respects the hard work these pros have put into their exasperating issues.

Independence

Retain and exude the professional independence about which we evaluators are so proud. This also is highly prized and is inherently valuable in a policy-making setting. If as a result of evaluator coaching, solutions to difficult problems emerge that most everyone can buy into, they will be happy to proclaim that an independent evaluator pointed the way. Even more, they are most likely to hire an evaluator to do a study precisely because they want a professionally independent assessment. They can easily obtain thoughtful assessments from stakeholders whose representative professionals are easily the competent matches of an outstanding evaluator. But such assessments are seen as biased and therefore unlikely to produce results that will narrow the gap among policy makers who have already struggled mightily to find feasible common ground on extremely difficult matters that have already been studied to death. They may view a competent independent assessment as a godsend.

How Can I Improve My Valuation Competence?

Gap Filling

Pick things to evaluate that are of interest to policy makers and stakeholders. Don't go over old ground. Generally speaking, the policy-making cadres are deeply immersed in their policy issues. Those who are at the table or advising those who are have read just about every relevant study on their issues—including national studies performed by independent offices like the Government Accountability Office, the Congressional Research Service, independent institutes and foundations, as well as disciplined studies of stakeholders and advocates. Similarly, state and local policy makers know their territory very well. But there are gaps not yet studied. That's where they will welcome an outsider's input. So find out what the gaps are and concentrate your efforts there.

This does not mean that the evaluator cannot choose the subject to be evaluated. However, unless the results are amazingly better than all the results the policy makers, stakeholders, advocates, and professional analysts have produced, it may be a while before any of them will perk up and pay much attention to an outsider's breakthrough insights.

Please note that this answer—focus on the gaps—may not be where a professional evaluator instinctively chooses to direct personal development. Many evaluators believe that their surest path to success is the mastery of new evaluation skills. That certainly is a part of it. But methodological shortcomings are not generally the first line of exploration of well-informed policy makers. With a few exceptions, they will assume that the evaluator is professionally competent, or will look for one who truly is. It is the policy-related subject matter that they are interested in. If later on stakeholders or advocates rip the evaluator's methods to shreds publicaly, it may be because they did not like the answer the evaluator came up with. But learning better methods will not prevent this outcome.

What Should I Not Do?

Bias

Policy makers may be suspicious of an evaluator's bias. In fact, it is hard not to be biased. Almost everyone, including evaluators, have political leanings. Evaluators need to recognize and mitigate their biases, not claim they do not have them. They need to search their own souls systematically to discover which ones they have, or at least the ones they exhibit. Then, they need to get them under control. For example, in choosing program options to examine, will the evaluator be likely to formulate both conservative and liberal solutions for examination? It isn't necessary to classify them as such, just to make sure they are all examined systematically, not excluded out of hand. It not only takes personal discipline to prevent the evaluator's natural bent from subconsciously dictating the general direction of evaluation. It also takes discipline to study and understand all the points of view and the competing analytic results already in the stew of ideas and solutions from which policy makers are eating. A competent evaluator needs to be able to articulate the pros and cons of the policy proposals already in play and do it in such a way that policy cadres of all inclinations will react by saying, "Yes, that is a fair and complete analysis." This is simply hard work, the absence of which will be promptly noticed. It is the starting point for evaluating the policy gaps that are so important to policy makers.

Disrespect

Today it seems like disrespect has become a stock in trade among policy makers. All the policy cadres—decision makers, advocates, stakeholders—can consult the hand they have been dealt and decide whether to play the joker card. But the evaluator cannot. Doing so will cause the irreparable loss of reputed independence. That loss will extend to the evaluator's entire practice. There really are no secrets in policy making. The word spreads; the bell cannot be unrung.

Conclusion

Evaluators have much to offer in the world of policy making, and policy makers appreciate it. But evaluators do not own the field of valuation. They will have to hold their own in a wide field of professional and passionate valuators. It is their broad command of valuation theories and practical methods, their independence, and their professional demeanor that makes them so valuable. The best way to preserve their independence and professional reputation is to be independent, relevant, helpful, and respectful. Doing so will yield improvements beyond imagining.

GEORGE F. GROB *is president of the Center for Public Program Evaluation and is a recipient of American Evaluation Association's Alva and Gunnar Myrdal Government Award.*

Patton, M. Q. (2012). Contextual pragmatics of valuing. In G. Julnes (Ed.), *Promoting valuation in the public interest: Informing policies for judging value in evaluation. New Directions for Evaluation, 133*, 97–108.

10

Contextual Pragmatics of Valuing

Michael Quinn Patton

Abstract

Valuing is context dependent. That is the cross-cutting theme of the chapters in this issue of New Directions for Evaluation. *This chapter highlights how each author emphasizes contextual sensitivity and adaptability in the valuing process and concludes with a personal interpretation of each author's evaluator context to add value to the wisdom and guidance offered by each.* ©Wiley Periodicals, Inc., and the American Evaluation Association.

Context matters. That was the theme of the 2009 annual conference of the American Evaluation Association. Valuing is context dependent. That is what the thoughtful and insightful contributors to this *New Directions for Evaluation* (NDE) issue conclude.

Debra Rog, in her 2009 presidential address, asserted that emerging from the long-standing methodological debates in evaluation has been recognition of the need for contextually sensitive evaluation practice, an approach that matches methods to the conditions in the context and the needs of the stakeholder.

> [J]ust as we opened the black box of programs through the use of implementation evaluation, we can navigate the "black hole of context" through the use of systems thinking and other approaches that explicitly examine the influence of the broader environment on programs and their participants. (Rog, 2009)

This issue opens the black box of valuing and helps us navigate the black hole of valuing by embedding valuing in sensitivity to context.

Contributions to Deconstructing Valuing Through Context Sensitivity

George Julnes, the editor of this issue of *NDE*, opens his introductory chapter by citing his work with Debra Rog (Julnes & Rog, 2007) on "pragmatic support for policies on methodology," reaffirming their caution that "efforts to be systematic sometimes have unintended effects, including premature constriction of useful diversity and a general inflexibility in crafting methodologies to match the needs of specific contexts" (p. 4). He continues by laying out his vision for the *NDE* issue: "To respond constructively to pressures for systematization while maintaining the needed flexibility to employ context-appropriate methods of valuing" (p. 4). He urges the evaluation community to be proactive in developing its own working consensus on valuing. That consensus, I would suggest, based on contributions to this issue, is that valuing must be understood as contextually embedded and dependent. Julnes argues that the different approaches evaluators use to make judgments depend on the contexts in which those different approaches are used. The challenge, then, is more explicitly understanding and matching the valuing approach and context.

He notes that some stakeholders will need more help than others in interpreting evaluation findings and making judgments (that is, valuing), so stakeholder capacity to engage in valuing actively and appropriately is a critical contextual factor. International and cross-cultural evaluation work "can sensitize us to cultural issues in aligning the evaluator role in valuing with contexts" (p. 12). In these suggestions, he is calling our attention to the fact that the relationship between evaluators and stakeholders is a critical dimension of context and he offers an insight, inspired by George Grob, which resonates in its parsimony and wit: ". . . valuation can be an evaluator contribution without being an evaluator monopoly" (p. 12).

Well said, sir. I value your valuation conclusion and urge readers to ponder its deep and broad implications both within and across contexts. This conclusion reaffirms and focuses on the challenges of contextually sensitive valuing and deserves emphasis through recitation here:

> [W]ithout sufficient coherent input from evaluators, government policies may dictate formal methods for judging value that do not reflect our understandings of best practices in specific contexts. To have more input that reflects more of the received wisdom of the evaluation community, we need to develop new frameworks for valuation that are more explicit about the strengths and limitations of different approaches in specific contexts and, hence, can be used to guide decisions about selecting and combining methods to fit differing contexts. (p. 13)

In his concluding chapter George Julnes offers the very new framework that he called for in his opening chapter—and it is a *tour de force*. He does an exceptional job of integrating brain research on how we make decisions, methods of valuing in relation to specific contexts, and practical guidance for distinguishing contexts. The challenge he takes on, and meets, is informed by pragmatism: "The pragmatic task for effective tool use is understanding effective combinations of tools according to context" (p. 113). Later he continues: "We need multiple paradigms to support our evolved cognitive capacities better—anything less is self-inflicted disability. This is the pragmatic project for assisted sense making" (p. 113). He offers a balanced approach explaining: "Perhaps the best defense for the desired balance will be policies that acknowledge the value of multiple approaches to valuing—not acceptance of all methods, but an endorsement of a limited subset with sufficient variety to cover the major valuing contexts" (p. 115). He then offers his valuing framework in a series of tables worth studying in detail.

I especially appreciate and value his use of complexity as a way of differentiating contexts, an approach consistent with other recent work on adapting evaluation to context based on complexity understandings (Funnell & Rogers, 2011; Patton, 2011). In combination, Julnes' insightful and useful framework takes us into new territory in understanding the important contextual dimensions of valuing. And be sure not to miss his brilliant and somewhat tongue-in-check appendix on "9.5 theses for pragmatic use and promotion of valuation methods in service of the public interest." Although some might remember Martin Luther's 95 theses on church reform, only old-timers will recognize this as a clever tribute to Lee J. Cronbach's classic 95 theses in *Toward Reform of Program Evaluation* (Cronbach & Associates, 1980); evaluation's newcomers, perplexed by the title, might be motivated to have a look at the original Cronbach et al. 95 reform theses, which are still relevant. I suspect Cronbach would be pleased with Julnes' additions.

Let me turn now to the contribution of one of Cronbach's evaluation peers, who has also expressed a long-standing interest in reforming evaluation, in particular, increasing understanding of and competence in valuing as central to our work. Michael Scriven opens his chapter with attention to how to validate values in a way that is both generally valid and *contextually sensitive*. Indeed, that is his goal:

> What I want to do here is to outline the logical infrastructure that makes it possible to claim that one can validate values, both at a general and a context-specific level, other than by direct deduction from other value premises. (p. 18)

He is emphatic that, contrary to classic assertions about value-free social science, "the meaning of valuable concepts [can be] be fundamentally context dependent, and still be entirely scientific" (p. 20). He goes on:

> . . . we can provide disciplinary and indeed scientific credentials for these imprecise, context-dependent, approximative concepts that are at the heart of evaluation as well as everyday communication. (p. 21)

Scriven concludes with attention to context-dependent rules of logic and valuing.

Marv C. Alkin, Anne T. Vo, and Christina A. Christie examine "The Evaluator's Role in Valuing." They observe that "different evaluation conditions will call for different approaches to valuing" (p. 30) and proceed to consider the influence of context on the evaluation process.

> As part of the total context in which evaluation takes place, and of particular relevance to our discussion on valuing, we consider the multiple theoretic perspectives that govern an evaluator's behavior. Each has within it an implied direction that valuing might take. We call this the *evaluator context*. (p. 31)

Attention to and understanding of *evaluator context* can help us open the black box and navigate the black hole of context sensitivity. It is worth noting that the construct *evaluator context* elaborates and deepens the category of *evaluator characteristics* that Alkin originally identified as important in his seminal and now classic study of evaluation use (Alkin, Daillak, & White, 1979) and carried forward in his practical guides to evaluation decision making (Alkin, 1985) and essentials (Alkin, 2011). He originally identified some 50 factors associated with use and organized them into four categories:

1. *Evaluator characteristics*, such as commitment to make use a priority, willingness to involve users, political sensitivity, and credibility
2. *User characteristics*, such as interest in the evaluation, willingness to commit time and energy, and position of influence
3. *Contextual characteristics*, such as size of organization, political climate, and existence of competing information
4. *Evaluation characteristics*, such as nature and timing of the evaluation report, relevance of evaluation information, rigor of methods, and quality of the data

These four categories or containers of situational characteristics remain a useful framework for analyzing, understanding, and making sense of *context*. In this issue, Alkin, Vo, and Christie define *evaluator context* (a specific dimension of evaluator characteristics) as the dispositions that may influence the way in which evaluators go about the valuing process. By evaluator context, then, they mean the *individual* evaluator's point of view, preferences, and approach to the valuing process. They conclude:

> . . . the evaluator engages in a process, a major element of which is assuring that valuing will occur. We must recognize the diversity of contexts, both evaluation context and evaluator context, and not insist that all evaluators perform valuing in one (presumed) "right" way. . . . Moreover, attention to different program contexts may lead evaluation theorists to modify their mode of valuing based upon the demands of the particular context. (pp. 39–40)

NEW DIRECTIONS FOR EVALUATION • DOI: 10.1002/ev

On the surface, the chapter by Brian T. Yates appears to be an argument for the importance of cost–benefit analysis as an approach to valuing. But he, too, is concerned about context sensitivity and, indeed, the phrase I've used to title this chapter, *contextual pragmatics*, is his, for which I thank him. (Thanks, Brian.) Yates argues that "major potential mistakes and biases in assessing the worth of resources consumed, as well as the value of outcomes produced" are most likely to occur "when the evaluation is limited in contexts examined or perspectives adopted" (p. 43). In particular, he asserts "that the price of a resource often is context-dependent" (p. 43). Then he turns to *contextual pragmatics*.

> Ignoring the *contextual pragmatics* of those resources available to, and used by, a program risks making attributions about the potential effectiveness of programs that may be more accurately attributed to the resources that were or were not available at the sites at which the program was implemented. (emphasis in the original). (pp. 44–45)

Yates goes on to argue that "most evaluations exclude meaningful information on the types and amounts of resources that were and were not available to the program in the context in which it operated during the evaluation. Particularly in times of increasing constraints on many resources needed by human services, program evaluations seem incomplete and even impractical unless they include the resources available to and used by programs in the contexts in which they try to operate" (p. 45). He also explains that "[p]rice is a function of contextual features such as demand by other programs and availability, and can be manipulated to create artificial scarcity or exaggerate apparent abundance" (p. 45). Later I'll return to the value—and limitations—of cost-benefit analysis, but let me quote Julnes' context-sensitive observation from his opening chapter: "[B]enefit–cost analysis is an appropriate valuation method in some contexts but should not be supported universally and uncritically by evaluators" (p. 8).

Stephanie Shipman leaves no doubt about her valuing of context. It's right there in her chapter title: "The Role of Context in Valuing Federal Programs." She examines how valuing done in federally sponsored evaluations depends on a range of contextual factors and explains that "[i]n the course of planning a study, GAO analysts review the program's authorizing legislation and legislative history, previous studies, and policy discussions to understand the policy context and identify available data sources, criteria, and measures that have been used before" (pp. 58–59). Shipman also emphasizes that to form an overall summative conclusion about a program's value, "the choice of evaluative criteria depends on the context of a particular decision" (p. 60).

In a similar vein, François Dumaine makes the importance of context explicit in his title. He focuses on the Canadian context for evaluation, specifically (and this is critical) the way in which the current federal government has formally linked program evaluation to its strategic review initiative. On this linkage between strategic reviews and evaluation, he explains:

> There is not a predefined process or methodology that federal departments must follow when undertaking their strategic review. It is up to each department to determine how they intend to address the seven questions and identify the 5% of lowest-priority, lowest-performing programs to be cut in favor of reallocations or direct savings. In this context, federal departments have had to learn by doing, creating their own templates and establishing a web of internal procedures and committees that have fed information to the highest levels of management within the organization and have had to build their case to be presented to central agencies for consideration and, ultimately, for approval. (p. 67)

Eleanor Chelimsky brings special sensitivity to and insights about how shifts in the national context affect evaluation. As one of evaluation's pioneers, she has observed more than a half-century of developments in approaches to valuing. Like Stephanie Shipman, with whom she long shared the organizational context of the Government Accountability Office (GAO), she emphasizes the importance of understanding the historical, political, and evaluative context of the subject matter of the evaluation. This contextual understanding informs and links to the kind of evaluation question being asked, which then determines what methods are appropriate to generate findings that can be interpreted and valued. She writes:

> The type of evaluation question posed . . . will largely determine which methods are appropriate for a particular evaluation, based also, however, on the historical, political, and evaluative context of the subject matter. (p. 78)

She then turns to methodological trends as a dimension of contextual pragmatics.

> Some evaluative methods have benefited from various periods of vogue in different government agencies. For example, cost/benefit analysis was an important component of the Department of Defense's Planning, Programming and Budgeting System in the sixties; randomized controlled designs were favored by the Office of Economic Opportunity and other agencies for social program demonstrations in the sixties and seventies (as well as more recently, by the Department of Education); and the case-study method was the rock on which the Government Accountability Office built its evaluations over a period of decades. (p. 78)

Essentially, Chelimsky documents that despite widespread lip service to *choosing* methods that are appropriate to the question, organizational history, culture, politics, and methodological fashion (what is in vogue) actually determine what methods are valued, required, mandated, funded, and "chosen"—chosen in the same way that bears choose to like honey. Later, I'll emphasize the importance of paying attention to Chelimsky's warnings about the single narrative as a dominant feature of our current national political context, but first let me complete our tour of contextual pragmatics in this issue's chapters.

Michael Morris calls our attention to the "potentially thorny problem of deciding on the 'one best' criterion to employ in a given evaluation context" (p. 86). He suggests that the pressure to settle on one best criterion has to be "finessed" and concludes that "the task of searching for the one best criterion is an ill-advised quest" (p. 86).

> [a]nalyses must be tied to the specific contexts within which these stake-holders are actually approaching decisions. . . . Analyses that acknowledge and explore how these dynamics operate within the context of specific valuation perspectives are sorely needed. (p. 88)

George F. Grob makes the world his context, a *World of Valuators*, a world in which evaluators are but one subspecies among *homo sapiens* engaged in valuing and evaluating. "[E]valuators have no monopoly on valuation" (p. 91). Or even oligopoly. Moreover, although we may presume to bring expertise on valuing to any given context where formal evaluation is to occur, we will have to prove our expertise, establish the value we add, if any, and show that we can be useful to our fellow human valuators.

> All of them—legislators, executives, managers, advisors, professional analysts of all kinds, advocates, policy analysts, social scientists, influential reporters and media personalities, and (of course) professional evaluators—are valuators. It doesn't matter whether evaluators believe that they are the only trained, professional valuators. All the other policy players just go ahead and valuate away. (p. 92)

> [Evaluators] do not own the field of valuation. They will have to hold their own in a wide field of professional and passionate valuators. (pp. 95–96)

Grob recommends being independent, relevant, helpful, and respectful. Based on his long, successful career working at the federal level, he emphasizes that the valuing process involves many stakeholders in which evaluation findings inform dialogue and deliberation but do not, by themselves, determine policy decisions. In essence, Grob's important insight is that evaluators should not expect policy makers to simply accept our findings because we carry the title "evaluator." Those with whom we work are, too, evaluators within their own contexts. And they will evaluate what we present to them. If they engage seriously with evaluation results and recommendations it will be because we answered significant unanswered questions, presented convincing evidence, and laid out practical solutions to difficult problems. Grob's reflections about evaluation being part of the deliberative process rather than determinative or domineering is consistent with research on use that has documented how evaluation findings are typically but one input in the policy making process: an important input, when well done, but still only one input as policy makers take into account diverse perspectives, conflicting evidence, and practical considerations (like budgets and politics). That is the federal government context for valuing and evaluation use and Grob knows it well.

The Personal Factor and Concrete Guidance on Becoming More Skilled at Valuing

Having established that context matters, let me conclude by adding that people matter. Utilization-focused evaluation emerged out of the discovery that the personal factor makes a fundamental and critical difference in whether and how evaluations are used (Patton, 2008; 2012). The personal factor has to do with understanding, honoring, and cultivating individual interest, knowledge, commitment, motivation, and capacity. The dreary world George F. Grob describes (dreary to me) misses those stakeholders who care deeply about being effective and/or supporting effectiveness, and embrace evaluations that can be useful in helping them actualize their values.

Evaluators are people too. It is true that this point is sometimes missed by those we encounter in our work. Our humanity may be missed because, as evaluators and valuators, we sometimes evoke fear, resistance, anger, loathing, or leeriness. Or, even more distressing, we evoke apathy and disregard. But, when we are sensitive to context and attend to the personal factor, we can evoke respect, appreciation, engagement, and, ignored at our peril, funding. With that as context, let me bring the personal factor into this review by telling you more about the people who are the authors of these chapters, how who they are and what they've done informs their perspective (the evaluator context of Alkin, Vo, and Christie in this issue), and why you, dear reader, whether novice or veteran, optimistic or skeptical, highly experienced or still in the early stages of valuation skill building, should pay attention to their personal wisdom and advice (which is not always explicit, but I will make so).

Author by Author Challenges for Reflection and Professional Development

Michael Scriven's name is hallowed in evaluation, appropriately so. I am writing this a week after Claremont Graduate College sponsored a celebration of Scriven's career and mammoth contributions. He presented a vision of evaluation as a transformative *alpha transdiscipline* that is recognized as a valued reservoir of knowledge and practice for evaluating and valuating. But what you need to know to appreciate his chapter in this issue is that he comes to evaluation from the philosophy of science and that he has spent his entire distinguished career battling the notion, deeply embedded in much of academia, especially in social science, that science is and ought to be value free. This notion was dominant in my own training as a sociologist and had to be shed for me to become an effective practicing professional evaluator. Scriven debunks the assumptions and premises of value-free social science.

Moreover, and this is critically important, he shows that valuing is fundamentally about reasoning and critical thinking. Evaluation as a field has become methodologically manic–obsessive. Too many of us, and those who commission us, think that it's all about methods. It's not. It's all about reasoning. That's why I repeat whenever I can the observation offered by Harvard Physicist Percy W. Bridgman, Nobel Prize recipient, 1946, for discoveries in high-pressure physics: "The scientific method, so far as it is a method, is nothing more than doing one's damnedest with one's mind, no holds barred" (quoted by Waller, 2004, p. 106).

So, let me highlight two key challenges from Scriven's chapter: Do you understand and can you articulate the logical fallacies in assertions of a value-free social science? Do you understand and can you articulate why this matters to the practice of evaluation?

Do you understand and can you articulate the logic of valuing and probative inference? Can you explain to the stakeholders with whom you typically work how to engage in making sense of findings and rendering judgments of merit and worth based on probative inference? Can you even explain it to yourself? If not, get busy. There is work to do. Time's a wastin'.

Alkin has devoted his distinguished career to studying evaluation use and distinguishing and illuminating evaluation theories—and theorists (the personal factor). Christie is a former student, now a professor of evaluation at UCLA, and Vo is a current student. Alkin has thought deeply about valuing for years and has imparted to his students a passion for understanding the connections among valuing, evaluation use, and evaluation methods, both as distinct perspectives and as interconnected dimensions of evaluator context (Alkin, 2012). The Alkin, Vo, and Christie chapter offers an opportunity for evaluators to think about their own personal evaluator context. Do not treat this as an abstraction or as a merely interesting and, perhaps, provocative intellectual construct. Examine and make explicit (to yourself first) your evaluator context. What influences the way in which you go about the valuing process? What are your theoretic dispositions as an evaluator? How does your individual point of view and preferences inform and undergird your approach to the valuing process?

One of the six essential competencies that undergird effective professional evaluation development is *reflective practice:* An awareness of one's program evaluation expertise as well as the needs for professional growth (King, 2007; Patton, 2012, Step 2). Are you aware of and reflective about your evaluator context?

Brian T. Yates is the treasurer of the American Evaluation Association and has served in that capacity for a number of years. He brings his concerns about and competencies in cost–benefit analysis to the decision making of the AEA board. He reminds us that cost–benefit analysis is a widely used and much valued framework for valuing. Of course, cost–benefit decision making is easy when one program achieves the same outcomes as another, comparable one, but at a lower cost, or achieves better outcomes at the same cost. Unfortunately, in my experience, those results are the exception. The tougher, and in my experience more common, case is where the higher-cost program also has better outcomes. Then the question becomes: Do decision makers place more value on costs or results? Often, what is supposedly cost–benefit analysis simply defaults to cost analysis, with lower cost trumping all other value considerations.

Stephanie Shipman has a distinguished career at GAO dealing with a broad array of kinds of evaluation employing the full toolkit of evaluation methods. She explains the importance, as part of design, of reviewing the program's authorizing legislation and legislative history, previous studies, and policy discussions, to understand the policy context and identify available data sources, criteria, and measures that have been used before. This is history as baseline context. Young and novice evaluators would do well to take note of the wisdom from this evaluation veteran about the importance of reviewing and understanding the historical context and origins of a program or policy as part of establishing the evaluation context. Too often, I find, if done at all, the baseline historical context is generated in a surface or cavalier way, relying entirely on one key informant's perspective (e.g., the program director or evaluation commissioner/funder). Dig deeper. Use multiple sources. Review original authorizing documents. Get diverse perspectives. Take the study of context seriously.

François Dumaine gives us a Canadian perspective on evaluation, and he is well qualified to do so. I fear that many American evaluators, being quintessentially ethnocentric, despite protests to the contrary, will skip this chapter because, well, it's about Canada. (You know who you are. Be ashamed. Be very ashamed.) I do a great deal of work in Canada. The Canadian Evaluation Society is the global leader in offering professional development and certification based on essential competencies (Canadian Evaluation Society, 2010). Dumaine portrays an approach to evaluation that is more fundamentally strategic than typical American approaches. His chapter invites us to reflect on how our evaluations are, or are not, connected to strategic issues that matter to decision makers.

Eleanor Chelimsky exemplifies evaluation excellence. In over a half-century of professional evaluation contributions, she has persistently called our attention to the critical importance of evaluator integrity and credibility

New Directions for Evaluation • DOI: 10.1002/ev

as key to evaluation use. She created and ran the outstanding Evaluation Institute at GAO. She knows the ins and outs of politics as well as anyone and far better than most. So, when Eleanor Chelimsky warns about the deteriorating United States political environment for evaluation and the deep dangers of "the single narrative," pay attention. As part of our commitment to promote the public welfare, we all need to become part of the chorus of concerned professionals sounding the alarm about the politicization of evaluation, especially in the form of the single narrative. Eleanor Chelimsky has seen and dealt with a lot of politics, of both the down-and-dirty and pretensions-to-higher-good varieties. When she says things are getting worse, be afraid. Be very afraid. And work to change the political context.

Michael Morris teaches evaluation ethics, writes about ethics, and has become an ethical lighthouse for the profession. His book on evaluation ethics is the go-to source for dilemmas of all kinds. He is too modest—and ethical—to cite (and promote) the book in his chapter, so I'll do it here (Morris, 2007). He offers four recommendations for enhancing evaluation practice with greater attention to and skill at valuing. Don't rush through that list. Savor it. Reflect deeply on it. Assess your own competencies and commitments in this regard. When someone with the experience, wisdom, and ethical grounding of Morris offers a short list of value-based, evaluative recommendations to ponder, become an evaluation user.

George F. Grob is a consultant to the American Evaluation Association Evaluation Policy Task Force. He has worked diligently to enhance the professional status of evaluation in the federal government. His leadership and work on the *Evaluation Roadmap for a More Effective Government* (American Evaluation Association, 2010) has been a significant and valued contribution to the profession. I'm going to give George the benefit of the doubt and suggest that his assertion of and praise for a "world of valuators" is diplomatically inspired and a result of bending over backwards to find value among the many politicians and bureaucrats he encounters in working on evaluation policy. I still think he paints a picture of evaluation as the new dismal profession. I offer these hypotheses to George: Low expectations for use breed low use. No expectations for use breed no use. High expectations for use? I urge all readers to try it and see what happens—if you conduct the evaluation in a way that genuinely adds value.

References

Alkin, M. C. (1985). *A guide for evaluation decision makers.* Beverly Hills, CA: Sage.

Alkin, M. C. (2011). *Evaluation essentials: From A to Z.* New York: Guilford.

Alkin, M. C. (Ed.). (2012). *Evaluation roots: Tracing theorists' views and influences* (2nd ed.). Thousand Oaks, CA: Sage.

Alkin, M. C., Daillak, R., & White, P. (1979). *Using evaluation: Does evaluation make a difference?* Beverly Hills, CA: Sage.

American Evaluation Association. (2010). *An evaluation roadmap for a more effective government.* Retrieved from http://www.eval.org/EPTF/aea10.roadmap.101910.pdf

Canadian Evaluation Society. (2010). *Competencies for Canadian evaluation practice.* The Canadian Evaluation Society. Retrieved from http://www.evaluationcanada.ca/txt /2_competencies_cdn_evaluation_practice.pdf

Cronbach, L. J., & Associates (1980). *Toward reform of program evaluation.* San Francisco, CA: Jossey-Bass.

Funnell, S. C., & Rogers, P. J. (2011). *Purposeful program theory: Effective use of logic models and theories of change.* San Francisco, CA: Jossey-Bass.

Julnes, G., & Rog, D. (2007). Pragmatic support for policies on methodology. *New Directions for Evaluation, 113,* 129–147.

King, J. (2007). *Essential competencies for program evaluators.* Retrieved from http://www .eval.org/SummerInstitute07/Handouts/si07.kingF.pdf

Morris, M. (2007). *Evaluation ethics for best practice: Cases and commentaries.* Thousand Oaks, CA: Sage.

Patton, M. Q. (2008). *Utilization-focused evaluation* (4th ed.). Thousand Oaks, CA: Sage.

Patton, M. Q. (2011). *Developmental evaluation: Applying complexity concepts to enhance innovation and use.* New York, NY: Guilford.

Patton, M. Q. (2012). *Essentials of utilization-focused evaluation.* Thousand Oaks, CA: Sage.

Rog, D. (2009, November). *Toward context-sensitive evaluation practice.* Presidential address, Annual conference of the American Evaluation Conference, Orlando, Florida.

Waller, J. (2004). *Fabulous science: Fact and fiction in the history of scientific discovery.* New York, NY: Oxford University Press.

MICHAEL QUINN PATTON is an independent evaluation consultant and former president of the American Evaluation Association.

Julnes, G. (2012). Developing policies to support valuing in the public interest. In G. Julnes (Ed.), *Promoting valuation in the public interest: Informing policies for judging value in evaluation. New Directions for Evaluation, 133,* 109–129.

11

Developing Policies to Support Valuing in the Public Interest

George Julnes

Abstract

The author offers a framework for supporting valuing in the public interest, informed by a pragmatic approach that acknowledges and defends the value of multiple approaches to valuing. With our multiple approaches understood as tools for assisted sense making, the task for evaluators is to understand the factors that lead some tools to be more effective for valuing in particular contexts. Factors addressed include the decisions confronting stakeholders and the needed complexity and precision of valuation. The result is a more systematic and yet responsive framing that balances (a) individual and social valuation, (b) algorithmic and holistic approaches to summative conclusions, and (c) the often-conflicting paradigms that structure other debates in evaluation. Tentative implications of this framework are suggested for the evaluation community, for government and foundation methodology policies, and for education and training. © Wiley Periodicals, Inc., and the American Evaluation Association.

E valuation is increasingly central to a more systematic and outcomes-oriented approach to public-sector decision making. With this success, however, come expectations that evaluation practice itself be evidence based, with governments and foundations encouraging use of

Patria deLancer Julnes and John Stevenson read earlier versions of this chapter and provided helpful feedback. I bear the responsibility for any problems that remain.

NEW DIRECTIONS FOR EVALUATION, no. 133, Spring 2012 © Wiley Periodicals, Inc., and the American Evaluation Association. Published online in Wiley Online Library (wileyonlinelibrary.com) • DOI: 10.1002/ev.20012

methods empirically identified as representing best practice. This pressure to be more systematic in using best methods was controversial when used to justify priority given to random assignment experimental methods for determining causal impacts (Julnes & Rog, 2007). Now, with increasing attention on using evaluation to maximize value for money in public-sector initiatives (Dumaine, this issue) will come increased pressure to be more systematic and deliberate in using best practices to judge the value of alternatives. This concluding chapter of this issue on valuing in evaluation provides a framework that addresses (a) selecting valuing methods that are appropriate for different contexts and (b) developing public policies that support making use of our multiple approaches to valuing to inform decision-making in service of the public interest. Situating this framework requires first introducing the pragmatic perspective animating this volume and the goal of being both systematic and responsive in guiding method choice.

Assisted Valuation in the Public Interest

To make decisions, to choose one path over another, is to make value judgments that one path is "better" than another. We make these judgments daily, hourly, with little concern. However, when the outcomes are important and the considerations complex, we rely on methods to assist us in these choices. Over time these methods of assisting our judgments have become more sophisticated as limitations of prior approaches become obvious, but all such methods, whether in program evaluation, policy analysis, or performance management, have basic similarities.

Primary among these similarities is that all approaches involve at least two steps. First, our methods analyze and valuate separately the major aspects or components of the situation confronting decision makers (often by distinguishing and valuing outcomes). Then, we aggregate, or synthesize, those valuated components into an overall value judgment that, in turn, supports decision making. The two kinds of aggregation required for public policies are (a) combining different criteria (e.g., cost, effectiveness, and intrusiveness) and (b) summing across all people who are affected.

Representing the Public Interest

This challenge of aggregation makes valuing in the public interest particularly complex, in part because there is no consensus on what constitutes a good society or what is really in the best interests of people. Valuing in the public interest is also complex because most initiatives create both winners and losers among the public. In that imposing costs on citizens is generally difficult for governments to justify, providing such a justification was the initial task of economic benefit–cost analysis (also called cost–benefit analysis), intended as yielding a "moral criterion [that] identifies the features of outcomes that make them morally better or worse than alternatives" (Adler & Posner, 2006, p. 62). A standard application of benefit–cost analysis is to identify the major outcomes of a proposed project, valuate these outcomes according to stakeholder values, often based on willingness to pay (as in how much extra people are willing to pay to be in districts with excellent schools), and sum all of the benefits and costs into a net value (or, when discounting based on the timing of these impacts, the net present value). This resulting number is interpreted as the *value* of the project, and the moral action, according to the Kaldor–Hicks utilitarianism logic, is to maximize value so defined.

There are many critiques of this approach (see Adler & Posner, 2000; Sinden, Kysar, & Driesen, 2006), with the general concern being what evaluators call construct validity—Does the calculated net value represent overall well-being? This can involve criticism that the preferences represented in benefit–cost analysis do not distinguish real human needs from superficial preferences or that the methodology does not consider the preferences of future generations that will live with the consequences of current decisions. In addition, valuation based on willingness to pay intrinsically favors the preferences of those having lots of money to pay. There is also concern that dictating policy from current preferences undermines the important ways that new laws and regulations (e.g., in the area of civil rights) can influence future preferences for the better. Related, accepting primacy of "maximizing net value" could change how people view and value their world.

The aspirations and challenges of economic valuation offer several lessons for the field of evaluation. First, economic valuation needs to be more fully appreciated and used by evaluators, with Yates (this issue) as an early advocate of this approach. Second, the thoughtful criticisms of economic approaches should make us skeptical of accepting any valuing methodology as the gold standard for this task. Building on this, the third lesson is the need to retain, and even defend, the traditional valuing methodologies in evaluation, such as checklists, surveys, focus groups, case studies, and evaluator judgment. These other approaches complement the insights of economic valuation, although there is little consensus on their relative contributions, nor on the contexts in which they are most useful.

Developing some consensus on how our available methods of valuing are differentially appropriate in different contexts is necessary for guiding policies on methods of valuation to be used in evaluations conducted in the public interest. Note that guiding method choice invokes additional applications of valuing: (a) because we value some outcomes over others, we value those evaluation methods that help us identify those outcomes, and so (b) we value policies that promote context-appropriate use of those methods—and so (c) we value dialogue in the evaluation community that helps develop those policies. To contribute to the dialogue needed for this policy support it is useful to remember the goals of a pragmatic approach to guiding decision making.

The Pragmatic Project

Evaluation has rarely, if ever, been conceived as a tool for discerning Truth. Rather, the focus is always more pragmatic—making better decisions in applied contexts. To develop a pragmatic focus into a larger project for evaluation, consider first what it is not—facile critiques often fabricate a "mythical pragmatism (which the real pragmatists scorned) that says 'It's true (for you) if it is good for you'" (Putnam, 1995, p. 51; see also pp. 8–12). Better to remember the evolutionary roots of pragmatism, wherein our cognitive abilities are viewed as having evolved to solve problems. The basic cycle involves having the requisite variety available to allow for selection of the most adaptive variations, and then a retention mechanism to preserve what is selected. In this framing, knowing what is good for you, or "what works," can serve, under the right circumstances and among other desiderata, as one criterion for guiding our evolving beliefs about what seems true. For example, the cognitive capacities that humans use to make sense of the world are suggestive of what the world *must be like* for these capacities to have evolved (as in, there must be enough regularity in the world, with past experiences having some relevance for the future, such that our cognitive capacities are adaptive).

Tools assisting capacities. This emphasis on evolutionary process is central to pragmatism, applied not just to our cognitive capacities but also to our methods of valuation, and to the frameworks we use to guide method choice. Accordingly, rather than burdening them with an impossible criterion of truth, think in terms of our theories, methods, and, yes, even evaluation reports as "tools" that support effective practice. Further, just as physical tools assist our natural capacities, so it is that our valuation methods assist our natural valuing capacities, and so it is that conceptual frameworks can assist our intuitive capacities for choosing context-appropriate valuation methods.

In this context, a pragmatic strategy (following Kant), is to say "As a being who makes value judgments every day, I am *of course* committed to the idea that there are true value judgments; *what must be the case if there are to be true value judgments?*" (Putnam, 1995, p. 43; emphasis in original). From our consistent experience with aligning methods with contexts, we can add, "What must be the case if some methods of valuing are better than others in specific contexts?" To understand this additional question, and hence improve practice, requires identifying and organizing some of the contextual factors that should influence our methods of valuing.

This emphasis on tools has implications for our understanding of the results of assisted valuation. For example, rather than view the results of benefit–cost analysis as a moral criterion, Adler and Posner (2006) present it as a decision procedure that yields a proxy measure for human welfare that is close enough to trust. However, this begs the question of how close is "close enough" for a proxy measure (Sinden et al., 2006). In contrast, pragmatists do not justify tools in terms of approximation to some ideal; instead, tools are valuable to the extent that they solve our problems. This is consistent with justifying benefit–cost analysis "as a way of counteracting predictable problems in individual and social cognition" (Sunstein, 2001, p. 233). However, the critical difference between the pragmatic position and those of most economists is the view that economic valuation, when used in isolation, creates its own "predictable problems in individual and social cognition." Reframed as such, economic valuation does not yield a proxy for welfare but rather serves as a tool that works best in conjunction with other tools. The pragmatic task for effective tool use is understanding effective combinations of tools according to context.

Capacities informing practice. If our conceptual tools exist to support our natural capacities, it is natural to consider what those capacities are. In the controversy over the appropriate roles for rigorous quantitative designs for causal impact conclusions, research on causal cognition in children showed how understanding our capacities can reframe the quantitative–qualitative debate. As Keil (1996, p. 243) summarizes, "[a]t this point, the evidence . . . strongly points to at least two sets of explanatory biases corresponding to two conceptual domains: a physical-mechanical domain that helps explain . . . mechanical causality, and a folk psychological domain that helps explain . . . belief accounts of causation." Conclusions about mechanical causality are strengthened by observing covariation, whereas the psychological domain involves understanding people's intentions. That is, evidence about our evolved capacities for causal understanding is consistent with the evolution of the quantitative (covariation) and qualitative (narratives including intentionality) paradigms in research and evaluation.

Viewing contrasting, and even competing, paradigms as manifestations of multiple cognitive capacities can and should be liberating. Rather than arguing about which evolved causal capacity is "better," we are better served by working to support each capacity and to understand how each supports the other in different contexts. Note well, this is not a reductionist claim that our methodologies should be derived from neuroscience, but it is an answer to the question of why we need multiple methodological paradigms: We need multiple paradigms to support our evolved cognitive capacities better—anything less is self-inflicted disability. This is the pragmatic project for assisted sensemaking.

Understanding our evolved valuing capacities can be equally liberating. Two examples include the evolution of cooperation and the evolved capacities of the human brain involved in rational and emotional valuing.

1. There is a growing literature on humans being predisposed for collective action (e.g., Poteete et al., 2010). Although a general tendency toward cooperation can be explained as adaptive for individuals in particular contexts, Nowak (2006, p. 1561) notes that "[s]election acts

not only on individuals but also on groups. A group of cooperators might be more successful than a group of defectors." For outcomes that affect the success of the group, therefore, coordinated action is important and so the value one person places on a set of outcomes can be contingent on the value placed on the set by others in the group. Communication and collective dialogue would likely lead to different valuations than would result from querying individuals in isolation. Further, if collective valuing led to effective action, our capacity for it could grow through an evolutionary process in which the success of collective action leads to predispositions for valuing cooperation, which lead to social norms and laws that make collective action even more successful (Tabellini, 2008).

2. Cohen (2005) examined the underlying mechanisms, and showed that different parts of the brain are involved in different aspects of valuing. When research subjects were thinking about receiving an immediate gift certificate, the emotional area of the brain (midbrain dopamine system, the nucleus accumbens) were active; when thinking about a gift certificate in the future, the rational prefrontal cortex area was active. Further, subjects who chose larger gift certificates in the future over smaller immediate gifts had more prefrontal activity.

To the extent that delaying gratification is viewed as a sign of maturity, methods of strengthening the dominance of "prefrontal rationality" are essential for public decision making. However, recent research in cognitive and neurosciences indicates that the emotional parts of our brain and their capacities are also critical to effective valuing (Damasio, 1995). The prefrontal capacities are most effective when there are a few, clear criteria to analyze (using the metaphor of serial processing), whereas the emotional capacities (viewed as parallel processing) are better at holistic processing of a multiplicity of less clear-cut considerations.

To understand the distortions that can arise from applying rational analysis to messy situations, Wilson and Schooler (1991) studied whether college students would replicate the taste preferences for strawberry jam of expert raters from Consumer Reports. A subset of 5 of the 45 jams tested by Consumer Reports was used. The students agreed with the experts on the two best- and two worst-tasting jams and had a correlation in ratings with them of 0.55. In a second condition, different students were first told they would have to explain why they preferred the jams they were rating. This emphasis on analyzing and justifying their preferences had profound effects on their ratings— the correlation of ratings between students and experts dropped to 0.11 and what had been the worst-rated jam for the experts ended up preferred by the students to the experts' highest-rated jam.

Taken together, these two examples suggest that different approaches to valuation should be more useful in different contexts. First, economic methods that posit the superiority of maximizing summated individual utility will be more useful in contexts where individual outcomes have little impact on communities (e.g., private consumption), whereas collective valuing will be more important when all are affected by social outcomes. Second, rational economic methods such as benefit–cost analysis will be more useful when the multiplicity of relevant factors can be adequately reduced to a small subset amenable to rational valuing; emotional valuing should be more necessary in ill-defined contexts with a multiplicity of relevant factors. This contextual view highlights the challenges in developing frameworks for guiding method choice.

Systematic and Responsive Tools for Valuing

Given this pragmatic view of the value of our alternative valuing methods, how can we be both more systematic in method choice and more responsive to contextual needs?

Systematic and responsive valuing. On the one hand, evaluators recognize the importance of evidence-based decision-making and so appreciate that this must apply as well to their decisions in selecting evaluation methods—in any situation, some valuing methods are better than others and should be used. On the other hand, evaluators also know that the complexity of contexts works against often mechanical efforts to derive the best methods for particular contexts—not only is there no one best method of valuing, there is also no one best decision-rule for selecting methods according to contexts. These two premises suggest the need for method-choice that is guided by contextual considerations but also allows for holistic judgments for aligning methods with contexts. That is, while we want to explicate rules to align methods with contexts, this "[e]xplication needs strong counter-forces to resist the tendencies to simplify" (Stake et al., 1997, p. 93). The goal, therefore, is not to develop a formal algorithm that derives preferred methods from contextual features. Rather, method-choice can be more systematic while also being responsive to context by identifying factors, sometimes referred to as pragmatic "design rules" (Alford & Hughes, 2008), that prompt us to consider implications for methodology.

Policies for systematic and responsive method choice. If evaluators are to base method-choice decisions for valuing on both evidence-based design rules and more holistic professional judgment, what sorts of formal evaluation policies would best support this balance? Perhaps the best defense for the desired balance will be policies that acknowledge the value of multiple approaches to valuing—not acceptance of all methods but an endorsement of a limited subset with sufficient variety to cover the major valuing contexts. If a working consensus on the nature of this subset of approaches could be developed in the evaluation community, it might be possible, as elaborated at the end of this chapter, to build on the success of the American Evaluation Association's Evaluation Roadmap for Effective Government to promote appropriate government policies on valuing methodology (Grob, this issue) and training programs (Morris, this issue).

Managing Context-Appropriate Valuation

If we accept that there is no one-size-fits-all best approach to evaluation, that context matters in selecting and implementing effective evaluation approaches and methods, then we need some guide in choosing methods for valuing that address the needs of particular contexts. However, if we also believe that contexts are sufficiently complex to resist simple decision rules (e.g., "if stakeholders disagree on program goals, use method X"), then we accept the need for a looser accounting of factors to be considered in matching methods to contexts. A sampling of these factors can be organized here into three stratified levels. The hierarchy of levels, shown in Table 11.1, presumes that you select valuing methods that (a) address stakeholder information needs, but that this requires (b) balancing approaches that are sensitive to our natural valuative needs, which in turn depends on (3) our understanding of social process needs (what underlying social processes are we trying to support?).

Matching Information Needs

In aligning methods with contexts, an important consideration is always the information needed for stakeholder decisions. Applying this to valuing, in what ways do information needs influence preferred valuation methodologies?

Matching stakeholder decisions and the complexity of valuing. Strategic design of evaluation requires evaluator understanding of the decisions that primary stakeholders need to make (Patton, 2008). For example, Weiss (1998) distinguishes decisions about midcourse corrections

Table 11.1. Aligning Evaluation Needs and Valuation Approaches

Evaluation Needs	Implications for Valuing
Information needs	
Types of decisions	Levels of complexity of valuing
Needed precision	Levels of measurement in conclusions
Valuation needs	
Balancing individual and collective values	Individual and group-based methods
Balancing algorithmic and holistic synthesis	Multiple approaches to aggregation
Social-process needs	
Development as process goal	Mechanistic and organic models
Paradigms privileging social problems	Strategic use of multiple paradigms

(generally, incremental changes to improve ongoing programs), program scale ("Continuing, Expanding, or Institutionalizing the Program or Cutting, Ending, or Abandoning it," p. 25), program funding continuation, choosing among alternatives, and testing new ideas. These decisions correspond to standard purposes of evaluation (Mark, Henry, & Julnes, 2000): Oversight and accountability (helping administrators and policy makers decide which programs are working well enough and which require attention), program and organizational improvement (addressed via formative evaluation), and assessment of merit and worth (overall summative judgments that support decisions on program continuation and selection among alternatives; a fourth evaluation purpose, knowledge development, is a mixed category not addressed further).

Table 11.2 illustrates that these decisions and associated purposes result in differing degrees of complexity of the value judgments required. Accountability and oversight generally compare activities and outcomes with established standards, which simplifies the valuation task for evaluators. Program and organizational improvement is moderately complex in that the overall value of the program need not be justified, but identifying "improvements" is nonetheless value based. In contrast, providing judgments of the overall value of a program, whether alone or in comparison with others, is quite complex. Not only must the full range of values important to stakeholders be included in the evaluation, it helps also to establish how the specific values relate to our larger concern with promoting the "public interest." This focus on the public interest increases the need to involve a meaningful range of stakeholders. In line with this dimension of complexity, Shipman (this issue) points out that GAO analysts feel competent to judge whether a program is in compliance with regulations, but defer to elected representatives to judge the overall value of a policy or initiative. Thus, increased complexity entails methods that support a shift in the locus of

Table 11.2. Decisions Driving Purposes and Complexity of Valuing

Practical Decisions	Evaluation Purposes	Complexity of Valuing
Which programs/policies need more attention?	Oversight and accountability	Minimal complexity; compare activities and outcomes with published expectations or regulations
What incremental changes will help?	Program and organizational improvement	Moderate complexity; presume value of program; operationalize improvement in terms of selected proximal indicators
Should the program be continued, expanded, or terminated? Which alternative is best?	Assessment of merit and worth	Complex; need understanding of the public interest; often requires diverse stakeholders and long-term indicators

Table 11.3. Variations in Needed Precision of Valuation

	Needed Level of Valuation		
Alternatives Evaluated	Categorical	Ordinal	Equal Interval/Ratio
Single Evaluand	Overall value: good	Levels of value: good and excellent	Amount of value: for example, $5,000
Multiple Evaluands	Multiple categorical claims	Ranking evaluands by value	Comparisons in amounts of value

valuing from program personnel to a more representative set of stakeholders and a shift from short-term indicators to more distal social goals.

Matching needed precision in valuing and levels of measurement. The types of typical stakeholder decisions also have implications for the nature of information needed to support them. For example, when evaluating a program, is it sufficient to report a categorical judgment that a program is good or is it necessary to distinguish ordinal levels of valuation (as in not good, somewhat good, good, or very good)? Further, there are also times in which decision makers want even more precise information, not only that a program is better than another, but also how much money a program will save or the actual net benefits of a program (actual numbers representing what are called *equal interval* or *ratio levels* of measurement).

Table 11.3 distinguishes between whether the judgment is to be about a single program or needs to compare two or more programs (with the thing being evaluated referred to with Scriven's term, *evaluand*), and illustrates that situations requiring more precision, in effect higher levels of measurement, will in turn require different methods of valuation. Some traditional methods of valuing, such as checklists, can be quite effective in supporting categorical and ordinal valuation, but are less so when more precise valuation is required (as with assessments of the dollar amounts of savings a policy change would yield). On the other hand, if a stakeholder judgment of "good" is what is required for decision making, presumably precise estimates from economic analysis may not be particularly useful (e.g., should an estimated value of $5,000 be considered good?). More generally, as Scriven (1993, p. 68) notes, "Different evaluation designs are usually required for ranking, grading, scoring and apportioning."

Addressing Valuative Needs

Meeting the information needs for valuation depends on proper approaches to understanding value. Among the many approaches available, the above discussion on supporting our natural capacities addressed: (a) the balance of individual and social valuing for the analytic task, and (b) the balance of algorithmic and holistic approaches to the synthesis of information into overall valuation. Each situation calls for its own balance.

Balancing individual and social judgments in valuation. Philosophers and others understand that we are at once both solitary and social creatures (Camus, 1958, p. 158). Accordingly, one distinction in the valuing methods evaluators routinely make use of is between those that are individual based and those that are group based. Individual-based approaches are those that do not require dialogue and interaction among stakeholders and include telephone survey methods and economic willingness-to-pay measures. Within this category there is an acknowledged distinction between so-called objective and subjective indicators of value, with some approaches making use of both, as when economic approaches use both archival data on willingness to pay and survey data from an approach called *contingent valuation* or in a survey measure of the value-based quality-of-life (QOL) construct "that combines measures of human needs with subjective well-being or happiness . . . [and including both] objective and subjective elements" (Costanza et al., 2007, p. 267).

Group-based, or collective valuing, in contrast, is based on stakeholder interactions. One distinction for collective approaches is whether these interactions occur among members of natural, intact groups (such as all of the employees in an agency division) or in what are called nominal groups, which involve people brought together only for the purpose of articulating stakeholder values. For example, Beywl and Potter (2005) present a responsive evaluation model that brings nominal groups together for group discussions.

Moore (1995, p. 36) argues this is an important distinction, wherein "both program evaluation and cost-effectiveness analysis define public value in terms of collectively defined objectives that emerge from a process of collective decision-making, whereas benefit–cost analysis defines value in terms of what individuals desire without reference to any collective decision-making process." Based on research on collective human action (Ostrom, 2007), we can expect (but should study systematically) collective approaches to be most helpful when an individual's valuing is dependent on the valuing of others (e.g., valuing inclusion of minority groups being dependent on the other groups' valuing) and when the diversity of values emerges better, perhaps with sharper distinctions, through dialogue than individual introspection.

Balancing algorithmic and holistic aggregation. Concluding that one alternative is better than another requires overall judgments based on aggregating values placed on the many activities and outcomes of a program and across the many stakeholders who are affected differently by the program. Many approaches to value synthesis involve some form of quantitative algorithm for aggregation. In the simplest cases this could be adding up the judgments on a checklist and reporting sums for relevant alternatives. More involved are benefit–cost analyses where the values ascribed to the major policy impacts are organized by their impacts on major stakeholder groups. Adding up all of these impacts across all groups yields a fairly defensible measure of overall value, the net value of the policy.

In contrast, some recommend and use a more informal, intuitive approach. For example, when using checklists, the synthesis could be based not on counting ratings but on a more holistic impression of the overall strengths and weaknesses of an alternative. Stake has argued for the superiority of holistic synthesis, noting: "We discourage the use of rubrics which assure a simple picture. We want to describe the complex 'values manifold' to be part of the summary report" (Stake et al., 1997, p. 97). In presenting a complex value picture to inform the holistic valuing of stakeholders, Stake promotes a subjective dialectic approach that prioritizes complexity, but at a cost of the transparency, replicability, and perceived objectivity of judgments that are important in many political contexts.

When might algorithmic or holistic syntheses be most appropriate? First, how important is it to stakeholders that the valuing appears objective? Some stakeholders may accept subjectivity as necessary for appreciating complexity; others may not. Second, recall from the neuroscience research described above, our "rational" valuing ability is limited to handling only a few factors at a time, whereas our holistic, "emotional" ability is less precise but able to process more information (Damasio, 1995). As such, are there only a few, clear criteria to consider in an evaluation setting? If not, then algorithmic aggregation is likely to exclude amorphous but important criteria that should inform decision making in the public interest.

Supporting Social Processes

Addressing stakeholder information needs and employing methods that support our multiple valuing capacities are important for evaluation. However, effective valuing also depends on understanding our long-term, or distal, goals. We can address this needed long-term focus by adding ever-more long-term outcomes to the evaluation plan, but an alternative is to consider effective, ongoing development as a type of goal. The implications for valuing include a focus on complex processes necessary for ultimate goals like social betterment, and a related focus on metatheories that might help evaluators be strategic in valuing programs in terms of different types of social problems in different circumstances.

Promoting social betterment. Valuing outcomes (e.g., rise in student attendance or rise in test scores) is more straightforward if there is a clear connection to the longer-term goals of most programs and policies. For example, getting people to stop smoking for a month would be judged as more valuable if we can presume that a high percentage of them will continue to not smoke for years, allowing reasonable confidence that the even longer-term, or distal, goals will be reached, that they will have fewer health problems, societal health care costs will decrease, and the world will be a better place.

This ultimate goal of a better world relates to what evaluators refer to as social betterment (Mark et al., 2000; Weiss, 1998). The lack of specificity in stating betterment as a goal is intentional—there is no consensus on the best distal goals, and yet we feel an intuitive sense of some outcomes being better than others. We assume, for example, that low unemployment rates are good overall, even though we know that there are some negative outcomes when work takes time away from the family. This suggests that any specific distal goal will only be an approximation of our ultimate goals.

An alternative, process-oriented approach is to view our ongoing development itself as the goal, with accomplishments (e.g., achieving stated goals) seen as milestones that serve as proxy indicators of effective ongoing processes. This move to a process orientation is seen in Seligman's (2011) transition from viewing happiness as the ultimate goal to promoting instead "human flourishing." Similarly, some philosophers of public policy (Rasmussen, 1999) promote human flourishing as the distal human goal. In the area of public administration this process orientation is seen in promoting the goal of creating public value (Moore, 1995), effectively asking administrators to step back occasionally to remember the connection between their immediate tasks and the larger issues they are to address.

Supporting complex social processes. If we are to embrace a process orientation, what are the implications for effective valuing in evaluation? Part of the answer depends on the complexity of the desired social process. We are accustomed to talking about some theories as being mechanistic and so of limited use in representing more complex, or organic, phenomena. Such talk addresses the metaphors that undergird our theories, a topic of interest a half-century ago in Boulding's (1956) delineation of a system theory that distinguished increasing levels of complexity, moving from physical systems, to biological systems, and then to social ones. His point is that things like feedback loops in our logic models are indeed improvements in complexity, but they involve only the cybernetic mechanics represented by thermostats, far lower in complexity than the social phenomena that we wish to understand. "Perhaps one of the most valuable uses of the above scheme is to prevent us from accepting as final a level of theoretical analysis which is below the level of the empirical world which we are investigating" (Boulding, 1956, p. 207).

This is not to say that mechanistic metaphors cannot be profoundly helpful. As Boulding (1956, p. 207) notes, "Because, in a sense, each incorporates all those below it, much valuable information and insights can be obtained by applying low-level systems to high-level subject matter." Indeed, one virtue of mechanistic metaphors is the clarity they provide, whether in economics or behavioral psychology. However, "[w]e should not be wholly surprised, therefore, if our simpler systems, for all their importance and validity, occasionally let us down" (p. 207).

This is important in that, despite all of the recent advances in areas called *behavioral economics* and even *neuroeconomics*, the economic vision of social process might remain fairly mechanistic as applied to the ultimate goals of human activity and to benefit–cost analysis in support of those ultimate goals. For example, Frank, Gilovich, and Regan (1993) conducted research showing that studying economics inhibits cooperation and leads people to be more self-interested in their behavior. Is it possible that, even with theoretical advances, the mechanistic metaphor underlying economics can support incorporating all possible outcomes valued by humans (preferences for equality, environmental health, and even world peace) and still need to be supplemented by other perspectives of human valuing? For example, the economic worldview, or paradigm, focuses primarily on increasing efficiency, with social conflict as a barrier to desired increases. Other paradigms, however, view some social conflict as essential for social betterment, that conflict suppression in the interest of efficiency is a barrier to social development. As such, economic valuation may oversimplify aspects of the desired human flourishing, leading to recommendations "that the representation of value not be simpler than the complex of judgments made" (Stake et al., 1997, p. 97).

Aligning paradigms with process needs. This notion that different worldviews conceive social processes differently, and so emphasize different problems threatening social betterment, needs to be addressed before systematic policies on valuation in the public interest are adopted and formalized. House and Howe (1999) made this point in delineating multiple paradigms for valuing. Because of the tendency to view our preferred paradigm as best, part of the difficulty in articulating policies for effective method choice for valuing is that we often are committed to unexamined worldviews that predispose us to privilege particular social problems and so reflexively adopt and use an unnecessarily limited set of evaluation methods.

Highlighting the influences of differing worldviews is the task of metatheories (defined as theories of theories). For the task of valuing, Deetz's (1996) reframing of the Burrell and Morgan metatheory provides a useful delineation of four paradigms that could guide policies on method choice. As shown in Table 11.4, each of Deetz's paradigms addresses a different problem and so accepts a different goal as necessary for desired social development. Given the importance of improving efficiency in most organizational settings, it is natural that administrators tend to approach their jobs along the lines of the economic-based normative studies paradigm. Natural, indeed, but what if there are other problems not as easily seen through the lens of the normative paradigm; what if being truly strategic in promoting social betterment requires input from multiple valuing paradigms?

If so, we need to promote the value of these different paradigms and resist efforts for government policies to privilege one and denigrate others. To help us position our evaluation paradigms in this framework, some of the House and Howe (1999) valuing paradigms are added as the bottom row of Table 11.4. Their preferred deliberative democracy model draws from several of Deetz's paradigms and so is different from his political view (critical

Table 11.4. Characteristics of Deetz's Four Paradigms

	Normative Studies	Interpretative Studies	Critical Studies	Dialogic Studies
Basic goal	Establish law-like relations	Display unified culture	Unmask domination	Reclaim conflict
Problem addressed	Inefficiency	Illegitimacy	Domination	Conflict suppression
Method	Nomothetic science	Hermeneutics, ethnography	Cultural criticism, ideology critique	Deconstruction
Metaphor of social relations	Economic	Social	Political	Mass
Organization metaphor	Marketplace	Community	Polity	Carnival
House and Howe typology	Postpositivist view	Radical constructivist view	Political–democratic view	Postmodern view

studies), but we can see that the other three paradigms correspond with the following House and Howe quotations (pp. 104–105):

> (a) "Post-Positivist (Value minimalist) (e.g., Shadish, Cook, & Leviton): Facts can be determined nonfoundationally but value claims must be tied to values of stakeholders in value summaries, 'X is good if you value Y.' *Evaluator role*: construct value summaries, accept stakeholder values. *View of democracy*: emotivist or preferential." [i.e., values as preferences to be reported]

> (b) "Radical constructivist (e.g., Guba & Lincoln): 'Reality' must be negotiated among stakeholders. *Evaluator role*: Mediate constructions of reality among participants. *View of democracy*: hyper-egalitarian (i.e., all views count the same in reaching consensus)."

> (c) "Postmodernist (e.g., Stronach & MacLure): Society must be liberated by disruptive acts. *Evaluator role*: deconstruct conventional notions and disrupt power relationships. *View of democracy*: hyper-pluralist (consensus not desirable, prolifereate diversity indefinitely)."

Deetz (1996) also presents his paradigms in the two dimensions shown in Table 11.5 to highlight fundamental similarities and differences. Two of the paradigms presume the possibility and desirability of consensus while the other two reject that, emphasizing "dissensus." On the other dimension, two views presume the validity of privileged (what Deetz calls elite) ways of valuing and the other two are more fundamentally stakeholder driven.

Table 11.5. Paradigms Aligning Valuing Methods With Primary Problems

	Source of Values		
	Local Voice	*Elite Judgment*	Aggregation of Value Claims
Dissensus	*Postmodernist view:* Problem: conflict suppression Valuing: advocacy for empowerment and voice	*Political view:* Problem: Domination Valuing: counter domination with impartial input for political process	Minimal aggregation
Consensus	*Constructivist view:* Problem: Illegitimacy Valuing: values inquiry to establish consensus	*Economic view:* Problem: Inefficiency Valuing: Kaldor–Hicks efficiency analysis	Aggregated accounts

Claiming the validity of each of the four paradigms does not require that each is equally important in particular settings or should be used equally often in funded evaluation. Rather, the metatheory reminds us that multiple social problems have historically been recognized and addressed as specified. For example, when efficiency is overemphasized to the point of disempowering people and threatening the social fabric, it may be particularly important for evaluators to give voice to the grievances of people, even if it does not lead to consensus (think of the perhaps self-serving criticism of the current Occupy Wall Street movement—"they can't come to any consensus") or to represent differing values in the political arena. On the other hand, when consensus is viewed as attainable and desirable, an evaluator could engage in value inquiry and aggregate the results to represent that consensus or, with true consensus on the problem of inefficiency, employ an economic perspective and make use of methods like benefit–cost analysis.

Implications for Evaluation Policy

The Deetz (1996) model is simply one possible framework for organizing multiple approaches to valuing; others are available and warrant attention. The larger point, however, is that something like this might be necessary for the evaluation community to fulfill its obligations to be both systematic and responsive in selecting, and justifying, context-appropriate valuation methods that truly promote social betterment. If we can endorse a framework organizing multiple, needed valuing perspectives, what might evaluators do to act on the implications of this view? Contributors to this volume show us some options.

Implications for the Evaluation Community

Evaluators generally accept that we have multiple methods in our collective toolkits and that methods must fit their contexts; this applies equally to methods of valuing. Evaluation associations could promote this awareness by being more explicit about valuing in their mission statements and guiding principles. For example, Chelimsky (this issue) criticized our tendency to accept a single narrative that reinforces our inclinations and biases. Morris (this issue) argued for evaluators to counter a similar narrow-mindedness by better articulating the major perspectives on valuing. For this it helps when journals like *New Directions for Evaluation* publish a volume devoted to the critical social theory paradigm (Freeman, 2010).

Another aspect of narrowness to overcome is the tendency toward orthodoxy in *who* should be making the value judgments associated with evaluation. Alkin, Vo, and Christie (this issue) explicated the diversity of stances on this question, and Grob (this issue) reminded us that everyone should be making value judgments: just as evaluators see themselves as considering multiple elements in arriving at a summative judgment, so must other stakeholders, with evaluation results being one of their multiple elements.

More generally, embracing multiple approaches to valuing requires attention by evaluators to how the different valuing approaches are to be combined and sequenced to best effect, something that Caracelli and Greene (1997) demonstrate with their mixed-method analysis of combining and sequencing quantitative and qualitative methods. Further, we need to appreciate how different contexts, such as different cultures, call for different approaches to this combining and sequencing of different methods.

Implications for Government and Foundation Methodology Policies

Several of the contributors to this volume recommended helping policy makers understand the need for appropriate valuing, with Grob (this issue) recommending coaching policy makers. Morris (this issue) agreed with the importance of this outreach, but recognized, too, the challenge in motivating policy makers to value alternative valuing practices. Chelimsky (this issue) argued for extending the successful AEA *Evaluation Roadmap for a More Effective Government* to address preferred valuing practices (such as guarding against intentional bias); consistent with her pushing back against accepting any single perspective, she also noted that federal agencies not only adopted single approaches to valuing but also differed from other agencies.

Shipman (this issue) methodically describes how different evaluation purposes are generally associated with different valuing approaches at GAO, and how GAO evaluators are constrained in their role in the political system—those wanting a critical social theory assessment of program value will never find it in a GAO report. Dumaine (this issue) adds practical insights on how changes in the role of evaluation in the Canadian government may be complicating the proper alignment of valuing methods with underlying government evaluation purposes. If we accept that serving the public interest requires multiple valuing perspectives but recognize that individual agencies will remain focused on specific perspectives, we need government and foundation policies that fund the other approaches to valuing in other ways. For example, McClintock and Lowe (2001) recount the disruption of an elite consensus of the "success" of welfare reform when welfare recipients were offered even limited voice at a conference: "Unfortunately, it was clear that the academic-policy culture and the welfare advocacy-service culture had different methods of discourse" (p. 14).

Implications for Education and Universities

Educators in evaluation-related fields have acknowledged the needed diversity in methods (e.g., requiring coverage of both quantitative and qualitative methods), but diversity in valuing methods remains underdeveloped. Morris (this issue) argues for developing a training package focused on the major valuation approaches. Once developed, this could support developing competence in multiple valuing approaches across the world. He also notes, however, that we know too little the actual impact of alternative valuing methodologies, suggesting the need for a research agenda within university evaluation programs to develop the needed empirical evidence. The university review panels on valuing bias that Chelimsky (this issue) recommends is another potential contribution from universities.

Implications for a Process Approach to Policy

Finally, if we accept that our ultimate public policy goals involve managing the process of our social development, and that we can have only glimpses of where we want this development to go, we need to act on our understanding that multiple valuing paradigms are critical to the process of error correction in our policies. Particular paradigms, whether economic analysis or constructivist consensus-building, offer many insights but become increasingly dysfunctional if systematically employed to the neglect of other approaches. Without diluting the virtues of individual paradigms, we need a social consensus that multiple perspectives of valuing are not only valuable but also necessary for desired assisted valuation. Such a consensus seems impossible in the current milieu where embracing one value stance seems to require denigrating all others, but this may be a special contribution for evaluators, serving as under-laborers promoting a more systematic and yet responsive multiplist framing of valuing in service of the public interest.

Perhaps one practical challenge to this multiplist framing is remembering, all-at-the-same-time, all of the insights that we have earned as an evaluation community. The introductory chapter of this volume quoted

Benjamin Franklin as suggesting a method to manage this all-at-the-same-time awareness, wherein "the whole lies before me, I think I can judge better, and am less likely to take a rash Step." Applying this assisted sensemaking to this chapter, the Appendix summarizes the main points in a set of nine (and a half; in homage to the 95 theses offered by Martin Luther and by Cronbach et al.) position statements, or theses.

References

Adler, M. D., & Posner, E. A. (2000). *Cost-benefit analysis: Legal, economic, and philosophical perspectives.* Chicago, IL: University of Chicago.

Adler, M. D., & Posner, E. A. (2006). *New foundations of cost-benefit analysis.* Cambridge, MA: Harvard University Press.

Alford, J., & Hughes, O. (2008). Public value pragmatism as the next phase of public management. *American Review of Public Administration, 38,* 130–147.

Beywl, W., & Potter, P. (2005). RENOMO—A design tool for evaluations. *Evaluation, 4*(1), 53–71.

Boulding, K. (1956). General systems theory: The skeleton of science. *Management Science, 1,* 197–208.

Camus, A. (1958). *Exile and the kingdom.* New York, NY: Vintage.

Caracelli, V. J., & Greene, J. C. (1997). Crafting mixed-method evaluation designs. In J. C. Greene & V. J Caracelli (Eds.), *Advances in mixed-method evaluation: The challenges and benefits of integrating diverse paradigms. New Directions for Evaluation, 74,* 19–32.

Cohen, J. (2005). The vulcanization of the human brain: A neural perspective on interactions between cognition and emotion. *Journal of Economic Perspectives, 19,* 3–24.

Costanza, R., Fisher, B., Ali, S., Beer, C., Bond, L., Boumans, R., . . . Snapp, R. (2007). Quality of life: An approach integrating opportunities, human needs, and subjective well-being. *Ecological Economics, 61,* 267–276.

Damasio, A. (1995). *Descartes' error.* New York: Penguin.

Deetz, S. (1996). Describing differences in approaches to organization science: Rethinking Burrell and Morgan and their legacy. *Organization Science, 7*(2), 191–207.

Frank, R. H., Gilovich, T. D., & Regan, D. T. (1993). Do economists make bad citizens? *Journal of Economic Perspectives, 10*(1), 187–192.

Freeman, M. (Ed.). (2010). *Critical social theory and evaluation practice. New Directions for Evaluation,* 127.

House, E. R., & Howe, K. R. (1999). *Values in evaluation and social research.* Thousand Oaks, CA: Sage.

Julnes, G., & Rog, D. J. (2007). Pragmatic support for policies on methodology. In G. Julnes & D. J. Rog (Eds.), *Informing federal policies on evaluation methodology: Building the evidence base for method choice in government sponsored evaluation. New Directions for Evaluation, 113,* 129–147.

Keil, F. C. (1996). The growth of causal understandings of natural kinds. In D. Sperber, D. Premack, & A. Premack (Eds.), *Causal cognition* (pp. 234–267). Oxford, UK: Oxford University Press.

Kierkegaard, S. (1938). *The journals of Søren Kierkegaard* (Alexander Dru, Ed. & Trans.). London, UK: Oxford.

Mark, M. M., Henry, G. T., & Julnes, G. (2000). *Evaluation: An integrated framework for understanding, guiding, and improving policies and programs.* San Francisco, CA: Jossey-Bass.

McClintock, C., & Lowe, S. T. (2001). Welfare reform and its enduring questions: What have we learned from evaluation research. In G. Julnes & E. M. Foster (Eds.),

Outcomes of welfare reform for families who leave TANF. New Directions for Evaluation, 91, 9–20.

Moore, M. H. (1995). *Creating public value: Strategic management in government.* Cambridge, MA: Harvard.

Nowak, M. A. (2006). Five rules for the evolution of cooperation. *Science, 314*(5805), 1560–1563.

Ostrom, E. (2007). Collective action theory. In C. Boix & S. C. Stokes (Eds.), *Oxford handbook of comparative politics* (pp. 186–208). Oxford, UK: Oxford University Press.

Patton, M. Q. (2008). *Utilization-focused evaluation.* Thousand Oaks, CA: Sage.

Poteete, A. R., Janssen, M. A., & Ostrom, E. (2010). *Working together: Collective action, the commons, and multiple methods in practice.* Princeton, NJ: Princeton.

Putnam, H. (1995). *Pragmatism: An open question.* Oxford, UK: Blackwell.

Rasmussen, D. B. (1999). Human flourishing and the appeal to human nature. *Social Philosophy and Policy, 16*(1), 1–43.

Scriven, M. (1993). Hard-won lessons in program evaluation. *New Directions for Evaluation, 58.*

Seligman, M.E.P. (2011). *Flourish.* New York, NY: Free Press.

Sinden, A., Kysar, D. A., & Driesen, D. M. (2006). *Cost–benefit analysis: New foundations on shifting sand* (Faculty Scholarship Series, Paper 373). Retrieved from http://digital commons.law.yale.edu/fss_papers/373

Stake, R. E., et al. (1997). The evolving syntheses of program value. *Evaluation Practice, 18,* 89–109.

Sunstein, C. R. (2001). Cognition and cost-benefit analysis. In M. D. Adler & E. A. Posner (Eds.), *Cost-benefit analysis: Legal, economic, and philosophical perspectives* (pp. 223–267). Chicago, IL: University of Chicago Press.

Tabellini, G. (2008). The scope of cooperation: Values and incentives. *Quarterly Journal of Economics, 123*(3), 905–950.

Weiss, C. H. (1998). *Evaluation: Methods for studying programs and policies.* Upper Saddle River, NJ: Prentice Hall.

Wilson, T., & Schooler, J. (1991). Thinking too much: Introspection can reduce the quality of preferences and decisions. *Journal of Personality and Social Psychology, 60,* 191–192.

GEORGE JULNES *is a professor in the School of Public and International Affairs, University of Baltimore, and his work focuses on improving evaluation methods, particularly for programs targeting disadvantaged and at-risk populations, and also on supporting government policies on evaluation that promote context-appropriate methodologies.*

Appendix: 9.5 Theses for Pragmatic Use and Promotion of Valuation Methods in Service of the Public Interest

1. Natural valuation is complexly contextual; assisted valuation is necessarily less so.
2. Evaluators must valuate, but so must other stakeholders.
3. Effective human valuing builds on both individual and collective, dialogic perspectives.
4. Analytic valuing corrects for holistic biases; holistic valuing corrects for analytic biases.
5. Effective valuing balances proximal and distal goals.
6. Ultimate distal goals are always processes (e.g., human flourishing, social betterment).
7. Our process models are usually less complex than the phenomena of interest.
8. Evaluation in the public interest always confronts multiple valued outcomes, but our paradigms privilege only a few.
9. The more systematic the use of our approaches to assisted valuation, the more systematically are their limitations revealed.
9.5. The above nine theses are to be prefaced with the phrase, "It's as if."

For this last half-thesis, consider Kierkegaard's (1844/1938, p. 134) perhaps rash critique of Hegel: "If Hegel had written the whole of his logic and then said, in the preface or some other place, that it was merely an experiment in thought in which he had even begged the question in many places, then he would certainly have been the greatest thinker who had ever lived. As it is, he is merely comic." *Seek systematization, but distrust it.*

INDEX

A

Abt, C. C., 80

Adler, M. D., 10, 111, 112

Aggregation methods: balancing algorithmic and holistic, 119–120; checklist approaches, 9; minimal, 9; quantitative, 9–10; social, 10

Alford, J., 115

Alkin, M. C., 1, 29, 31, 36, 37, 41, 45, 100, 104, 105, 125

American Evaluation Association (AEA): Educational Accountability public statement (2006) issued by, 86; *Evaluation and Oversight of Health Care Reforms in the House Discussion Draft Bill* (2009) by, 86; Evaluation Policy Task Force (2006) of, 87; *An Evaluation Roadmap for a More Effective Government* by, 79, 82, 86, 107, 116, 125; five modest recommendations offered to, 87–89; Guiding Principle of Responsibilities for General and Public Welfare by, 87; Guiding Principles Training Package of, 89; history of efforts to improve evaluation by, 85–87; professional standards supported by, 58

American Evaluation Association Evaluation Policy Task Force, 107

Aos, S., 47

Arendt, H., 82

Arrow, K. J., 9

Assisted valuation of evaluation: description of, 4; essentials of, 4–5; possibility of warranted valuation, 5–6

B

Bardach, E., 7, 9

Barkaoui, K., 45

Behavioral economics, 121–122

Bell, W. J., 5, 6

Benchmarking, 58

Berlin, I., 7

Beschloss, M., 81

Beywl, W., 119

Boruch, R., 38

Boulding, K., 121

Bridgman, P. W., 105

Bureau of Indian Affairs, 80

C

Campbell, D., 13

Camus, A., 119

Canadian Evaluation Society, 106

Canadian government: *Directive on the Evaluation Function* of, 69; evolving role of program evaluation in, 67–69; *Financial Administration Act* of, 68; implementing the new evaluation requirements, 69–70t; long-term impact on evaluation process of the, 72–73; Management Accountability Framework introduced by, 67;

Policy on Evaluation implemented by, 68–69; Strategic Review initiative of, 65–74; Treasury Board of Canada Secretariat of, 66, 67, 68, 74

Caracelli, V. J., 125

Carter, D. E., 44

Carver, R., 77

Chelimsky, E., 2, 50, 77, 78, 81, 82, 83, 102, 106–107, 125

Christie, C. A., 29, 31, 36, 41, 45, 100, 104, 105, 125

Cohen, J., 114

Collins, J. L., 87

Consumer Reports evaluations, 114

Context. *See* Evaluation context

Context-appropriate valuation: addressing valuation needs, 118–120; balancing algorithmic and holistic aggregation in, 119–120; balancing individual and social judgments in, 119; decisions driving purposes and complexity of, 117t–118; examining issues related to managing, 116; matching information needs, 116t–118; supporting social processes in, 120–124t; variations in needed precision of valuation, 118t. *See also* Evaluation context

Contextual pragmatics: description of, 101; summarizing individual author reflections on, 101–104. *See also* Evaluator context

Contingent valuation, 119

Cook, T. D., 7

Coryn, L. S., 12

Costanza, R., 119

cost/benefit studies, 78, 101

Cousins, J. B., 37

Critical inference: classical definition of, 25–26; evaluation supported by, 24–25

Cronbach, L. J., 13, 32, 33, 35, 99, 127

Cullen, A. E., 12

D

Damasio, A., 114, 120

Deetz, S., 122, 123

Deetz's four paradigms model, 122–123t, 124

Department of Finance Canada, 66

Department of Justice Canada, 69

Directive on the Evaluation Function (Canada), 69

Doshi, J. A., 48

Driesen, D. M., 111

Drummond, M. F., 49

Dumaine, F., 2, 47, 65, 75, 101–102, 106, 110

E

Edwards, W., 10

Einstein, A., 20, 24

Eisner, E., 38

Evaluation: definition of, 3; increasing importance to public-sector decision making by, 109–110; increasing pragmatism in, 112–115;

NEW DIRECTIONS FOR EVALUATION

ORDER FORM SUBSCRIPTION AND SINGLE ISSUES

DISCOUNTED BACK ISSUES:

Use this form to receive 20% off all back issues of *New Directions for Evaluation*.
All single issues priced at **$23.20** (normally $29.00)

TITLE	ISSUE NO.	ISBN

Call 888-378-2537 or see mailing instructions below. When calling, mention the promotional code JBNND
to receive your discount. For a complete list of issues, please visit www.josseybass.com/go/ev

SUBSCRIPTIONS: (1 YEAR, 4 ISSUES)

☐ New Order   ☐ Renewal

U.S.	☐ Individual: $89	☐ Institutional: $295
CANADA/MEXICO	☐ Individual: $89	☐ Institutional: $335
ALL OTHERS	☐ Individual: $113	☐ Institutional: $369

Call 888-378-2537 or see mailing and pricing instructions below.
Online subscriptions are available at www.onlinelibrary.wiley.com

ORDER TOTALS:

Issue / Subscription Amount: $ _____

Shipping Amount: $ _____
(for single issues only – subscription prices include shipping)

Total Amount: $ _____

SHIPPING CHARGES:	
First Item	$6.00
Each Add'l Item	$2.00

(No sales tax for U.S. subscriptions. Canadian residents, add GST for subscription orders. Individual rate subscriptions must be paid by personal check or credit card. Individual rate subscriptions may not be resold as library copies.)

BILLING & SHIPPING INFORMATION:

☐ **PAYMENT ENCLOSED:** *(U.S. check or money order only. All payments must be in U.S. dollars.)*

☐ **CREDIT CARD:** ☐ VISA ☐ MC ☐ AMEX

Card number _____ Exp. Date _____

Card Holder Name _____ Card Issue # _____

Signature _____ Day Phone _____

☐ **BILL ME:** *(U.S. institutional orders only. Purchase order required.)*

Purchase order # _____
Federal Tax ID 13559302 • GST 89102-8052

Name _____

Address _____

Phone _____ E-mail _____

Copy or detach page and send to: **John Wiley & Sons, One Montgomery Street, Suite 1200, San Francisco, CA 94104-4594**

Order Form can also be faxed to: **888-481-2665**

PROMO JBNND